# *The Book Of Being – Effortless Reality Creating With or Without The Law of Attraction*

I0417366

Trevor Emdon

ISBN-10:1466214694
ISBN-13:978-1466214699

# DEDICATION

This book is dedicated to my first great teacher, my mother, Esther Dorothy Emdon, who left this world in 1966 when I was nine years old.

# CONTENTS

# The Book Of Being

# ACKNOWLEDGMENTS

Every book I guess owes its existence to a small army of people. I can't think of a way to ever end my list, so I'm going to name the three who come to mind most often and hope those whom I have left out will forgive me.

First, my fabulous wife Ana who liberated me to express myself in whatever way I felt the need and who loves me unconditionally for who I am. There is no greater treasure in my life.

Second is my dear friend, Rik Lambert, whose excitement about this book spurred me to complete it also needs special mention.

Finally, I want to acknowledge the works of Dr. Wayne Dyer whose books and talks have, more than anyone else's in the last fifteen years, enabled me to see, feel and connect with the Divine Spirit that I am and which is the true Source and inspiration for this book.

# PREFACE

If you purchased this book yourself, (as opposed to being given it or acquiring it in some other way), you probably will have found it in the "self help" section of the book store.

That would be entirely appropriate because it is about helping yourself. Helping yourself to life and all its abundant riches – love, joy, material wealth, vibrant health, success and happiness.

It's an impressive menu and perhaps a little daring for a single volume to tackle so many weighty subjects, you might be thinking. But you will be pleasantly surprised because, as you will shortly discover, the keys to all of those things are really all the same. It's a master key – or a small set of them to be strictly accurate, that once acquired will open the door to anything, any way of life, any opportunity you desire.

You may have picked up or opened this book out of some sense of curiosity too, because I have written it for the sceptic, even the cynic. Not only that, but there is very little that is required of you to achieve the outcomes I have promised other than to read the book itself.

As I write this in 2011, "the law of attraction" has been a "bandwagon" for a few years now, and most especially since the release of a DVD and subsequent book in 2006 entitled "The Secret." If you haven't seen or read "The Secret" I can tell you, without fear of giving anything away, that the "secret" is that we can create our own destiny by use of the law of attraction.

Maybe you've heard of it, maybe you haven't. It matters little, but I do imagine you have come across the notion before. A hundred years or so ago the same concept was called "The Science of Mind." And the idea has surfaced in many guises since Biblical and even pre-biblical times.

You and I, along with a few billion other people, have not, however, grown up in a world where that concept is easily accepted. Although quantum science has been bearing out the metaphysical and mystical claims that have echoed down through the centuries, it has still done so rather kicking and screaming. Quantum logic – if that isn't an oxymoron – just wasn't supposed to show up this way!

Besides, most of us are not quantum scientists. I most certainly am not. I've read a handful of books for the lay person on the topic and seen a few TV documentaries, but that hardly qualifies me to put up a scientific argument. I can only quote what others have said.

It was, then, without formal training in science and with a high degree of personal scepticism regarding metaphysical claims that I set about putting my own life in order. I actually started this, without realising that was what I was doing, aged thirteen. (I am now fifty-four).

What I was interested in, then as now, was getting results. I wanted to have an all round better experience of life than the one I was having. I wanted not to worry and fret about money. I wanted not to feel that love was something that only happened in Hollywood movies. I wanted to write for a living because expressing myself through this medium – along with public speaking, of which I have never had a shred of fear – is what I instinctively knew I was born to do.

I could not understand why I was "forced" to go to work to do things that were meaningless and soul-less to me at times. Or why girlfriend after girlfriend abandoned me, or why lovely women just only ever wanted to be my friend and not my lover.

(Can you hear the violin strings yet? I'm sorry – I didn't mean to nauseate you!)

The point I want to make here is that I, like millions of others, blamed everyone else for my misfortunes. Life was just set up to be against me, it seemed. It was a very long time before I even got to the point of accepting that I was, every time and without exception, the common denominator in every thing – good or bad – that happened to me.

Even taking that notion on board, I still had to then figure out how I could change, how much effort change would take, and having once gone through the pangs of making change, whether any of it would, in the end, make the slightest difference to my fortune – or lack thereof!

To cut to the chase, I made a meal of it. Some might even say I made a "pig's ear" of it – although why those poor creatures' audio organs deserve that reputation I'm never sure.

So, what you're about to read I didn't make up and I didn't figure out yesterday. You don't need science or metaphysics for it to work, and the reason I say you don't need to do much is because life doesn't happen out of *doing*. It happens out of *being* as you will see – and hence the title of this book.

You still need to take action, but it becomes effortless action which feels like fun. Life becomes an experiment and full of wonder. (Do you remember those feelings from childhood? If you don't, go and find a child to watch!)

We are taught, most of us, not to be selfish. I would certainly agree that it is in no one's interest that you should be mean, but selfishness is a whole different ball game! Looking after yourself – finding, being and staying on the path that gives you the most joy will mean also that you have the most to give back.

You will love life and you will be loved for your love of life and for the lovely *selfish* being that you are.

And life becomes easy.

And very, very good.


### The Reason For All This

What is the point of all this, I used to wonder, if life is a mere blip between two eternities of nothingness - and all the things I do before eternity returns are things I don't like?

I was, perhaps, a precocious teenager but I can't remember a time when I didn't have thoughts of that nature.

If there's one value I hold in the highest esteem, it would be that each and every human – indeed every creature – has the right to follow his or her heart and live untroubled by rule-makers, prejudices and bureaucrats.

I am fully intending to show you how *you* can live your life in just the way you want it. I am giving you, if you like, the keys to the prison that you will discover is, however inadvertently, of your own making.

This prison is made of fears and anxieties. Among the most primal of these fears are that each of us is a separate entity who showed up here randomly, and that we can only exist for the merest fraction of a nano-second between two eternities. Moreover, the myth goes, we are insignificant beings on an insignificant and random planet which just happens, by the most incredible series of improbable coincidences, to support life. To date, we seem to be the only one.

Such notions will fill your days with worries about your own life as well as the future of our species and the planet itself. It renders you meaningless and the universe dangerous and hostile. Count yourself lucky to exist and make as few mistakes as possible and you might last a handful of decades. If you're extra good, when you get to the eternity that is to follow you won't be too badly punished!

Instinctively, you and I know this is nonsense! This is the thought-prison that gives you a sense of futility, perhaps even meaninglessness, about life in general and maybe, at times, (although I would hope not too often), yours in particular.

It gives rise to cynicism and it kills dreams. It may have already brought your own to near-destruction, and if you have children, you are in danger of speeding the fading of theirs too. After all, you will rationalise, you don't want them to be disappointed, do you? And you know as well as any parent: disappointment hurts.

My own father, who loved me very much, did it to me. He'd been a professional singer – a career he'd loved before I was born – but when I showed intention to take my singing and guitar playing "on the road" during my teen years, he warned me, with every kind intention, not to rely on "showbiz" as my meal ticket.

It wasn't unfair, but at the time I wanted encouragement. What I got was a burst bubble. I struggled on for a while after that, but the fear and the desire to please my father won out, and my guitar playing and singing became a hobby, which it still is to this day. But when I play, I still fantasise about, (and talk to), that imaginary crowd!

You won't kill dreams if you believe in your own. To do that you have to first believe in yourself. Furthermore, it helps if you believe that there is some kind of benign force that will support you – be it a fairy godmother, God, or just that the universe is a friendly place.

All of these things I had to discover for myself. Not only their whereabouts but also what each one was. It is only now, retrospectively, that I am able to identify what each stepping stone of my path has been and how much I needed to find it before I could reach, often groping and fumbling in the dark, for the next one.

You will not have to do that because I have illuminated the path for you in this book. You will be able nimbly to leap from stepping stone to stepping stone at lightning speed, (compared to me at any rate), and find the freedom and the joy that is your birthright.

Variety is not only the spice of life, it *is* life. If there was no contrast, if everyone was the same – sharing beliefs and cultural mores, values and tastes, we would have no inventions, no art, no *love* because how could you feel anything for someone when the next stranger would be exactly the same as your present lover?

Without our differences we would also have no sense of self or personal identity. We need comparison to know who we are too. And so I come full circle in the sense of saying that to dismiss or stand in prejudice against any individual, creed, race, belief system or anything else would render life absolutely pointless. It would also render me – and anyone who indulges in it – stupid. Because they've missed the whole point!

You cannot be happy by eliminating or avoiding everything and anyone who doesn't share your way of being and living in the world!

You get happy by being all of who you can be and enhancing the ability of others to do the same for themselves in their own way.

And that is what this book is about. It's what it's for. And it's why you are here reading it.

Whoever you are, it is a privilege to know you through these pages. Enjoy your journey – the part we're about to share and the rest of it when we part company too

Trevor Emdon.

Exeter, Devon. April 2011.

# 1: The Wondrous Trick

*"Sitting quietly*
*Doing nothing*
*The grass grows by itself."*

*- Zen Haiku.*

In 1988, my thirty-second year on this planet, I was shown a wondrous thing. I learned that by simply changing my view of something – literally – *inside my head* – my feelings about that thing would instantly change.

I treated this discovery something like a party trick, like a child who has discovered that he can go cross-eyed and that doing so has a marked effect on the grown ups.

Going cross-eyed, (something I can't do to this day), seems to make people laugh. But showing them how to change their thoughts alters their *lives*.

I was learning how to be a practitioner of something called NLP, or "Neuro Linguistic Programming" to give it its full title, and the wondrous "party trick" led to eye-popping and mind-boggling discoveries. (Although I have to confess I didn't discover them – I was taught them!)

I could permanently fix phobias in minutes. I could have people quit smoking in under two hours – and never go back to it. I could teach nervous individuals how to speak in public or ask someone gorgeous for a date.

My own life, however, remained somewhat messy. My love life was either non-existent or turbulent. Over the next decade I would go through two marriages and an equal number of divorces. Money seemed always and forever in short supply and acquiring more was as elusive for me as trying to sail to the horizon. I was frequently lonely and sometimes secretly and privately angry. Life wasn't supposed to be like this. And having a party trick or two up my sleeve didn't compensate or bring the joy I so badly sought.

I was working as a psychiatric nurse, for which I'd trained in the 1970s, and I had started to outgrow the job. It paid the bills, and it had its rewards, (and social life), but I knew I had so much more potential to fulfil in this lifetime. I wasn't about to do that, however, whilst I was heartbroken and broke.

In the early 90s my life and I almost fell apart entirely. My first marriage, which had been a nightmare for both my wife and me, ended amid a lot of fury and pain. It also left me grieving the loss of daily contact with my recently born son. When a new and very joyful relationship failed a few months after the end of my marriage, I hit rock bottom.

I simply wanted to die. I didn't dare to try that myself – I figured if I wasn't able to manage life I doubted I would be any good at ending it. But I did ask to be taken away from all of *this*.

Ask and it is given, they say. I was whisked away from all of *that* within days. Not only did my employer give me some paid time off (they actually *told* me to take some leave since I was barely functioning at any useful level), but no fewer than three teachers appeared in quick succession who all gave me the same message which was:

*We create our own reality.*

Of course I didn't want to have to accept responsibility for the terrible mess I felt my life was in. But I *did* want the power to create and to sculpt a new life for myself. A life that would be filled with love and joy and financial success too. A life where I could do what I love and be handsomely rewarded for it with love, with happiness and with material wealth.

I always sensed and believed at a gut level that we are meant to follow our dreams and to turn them into reality, and here at last were people who were not only showing me how to do it, but were themselves living examples that it can be done.

As I began to put into practice what I was learning about the new metaphysics one idea kept cropping up over and over again. That was the idea that it is how we think and feel that determines what results we get far more than what we do. To me this was a thrilling revelation! Had I not been taught in detail how to change thoughts and feelings back in 1988? I already knew this!

I felt like Dorothy in "The Wizard Of Oz" when she learns that her shoes would have taken her back to Kansas all along.

From then on, I experimented with applying the skills of NLP – which is an incredibly powerful set of tools for producing rapid and permanent change – to the principles of metaphysics which states that we can create our lives and circumstances according to our own design and wishes.

In other words, you can design your own destiny, and have that destiny show up in spades!

The more I applied my ideas, the more they worked. Today I am happily married – a phrase I once joked was a contradiction in terms. I live in rural England in an area of the country I will be perfectly happy to spend the rest of my days in. Money shows up regularly and always in amounts greater than I need.

And here I am, doing one of the things I've always loved – writing a real and proper book that can and I'm sure will positively impact lives. I hope yours will be one of them.

I privately nicknamed the blend of NLP and metaphysics I inadvertently created, Supertherapy." Not only did it allow me to bring about permanent change both in myself and in others, but it can also penetrate to the deepest levels of personality and the spiritual self.

This is not a "band aid" that covers up pain or enables you to cope like a crutch that helps you to walk with a broken leg. It will enable you to change your very *being* – who you are. You can grow, comfortably and at a speed that works for you, and most powerful of all, once you have mastered the principles you'll need no outside guidance.

Applying "Supertherapy" is simple, really simple because there's very little to *do*. You tweak a few bits and pieces in yourself, and as long as you're consistent, change will happen around you. Understanding it isn't difficult either, and really almost isn't necessary. Nevertheless, I've put a lot of background in the book for a most important reason: if you don't understand it you won't believe it!

If you don't believe it will work then you won't try it out, and your life will continue to be much the same as it is now, except you'll be a little older than when you began this book.

That would be pointless.

The wonderful spiritual teacher and writer Dr. Wayne W. Dyer says it best:

*"You don't attract what you want, you attract who you are."*

And if that doesn't sum up "being" and not "doing" then I don't know what does! You are, after all, a human *being* not a human *doing!*

So let's begin by having a quick overview of the principles of my "Supertherapy" and then you'll understand why the title of this book is "The Book Of Being."

# 2: Your First Thought

It's Monday morning. Your alarm clock has just woken you from a warm and deep sleep and shocked you into the realisation that another week is beginning.

What is your first thought?

Are you pleased that it's Monday? Or frustrated?

What mood are you in as you begin to force your tired body out of the bed?

Most importantly, who or what is controlling your thoughts and your mood?

Is it the situation? Your responsibilities to your self, family, boss, company ... are they all responsible for the way you feel right now?

Maybe it's your history. You had a bad upbringing or you never completed your further education, perhaps. You were bullied at school, were you? Oh, is that what dictates the mood you wake up in on this Monday morning?

Life's a drudgery. You have a dull job and you don't have high hopes for promotion or advancement in the near future. *That* must be what accounts for your not-so-great mood, surely?

Or is it just that you didn't have as much sleep as you would have liked?

Of course, you may have a reason I haven't covered here.

Let us accept, at least for the time being, that your first thought is kind of on autopilot. It just pops into your head. Okay, we'll take that on board.

But your second thought *isn't*. You can catch yourself thinking and feeling things that make you feel bad or helpless. (Why would anyone listen to the news as soon as they wake up? Peppered with doom and gloom-mongering as it is, how is that going to help you? More to the point, how are you going to influence any of the situations you hear about? Certainly not by feeling worried and stressed and helpless!)

When I say you can catch yourself, I mean you are self aware. There is a you that thinks thoughts! (We'll talk in depth about this later). The "you" that thinks the thoughts can *choose* a different thought.

So what?

So *everything!*

When you choose to feel good and positive and grateful and happy and loving and generous and talented and ... and ... *gorgeous* on demand life is good because life *feels* good.

*You* feel good.

When you feel good, your good feelings are infectious and you make other people feel good just by being happy and smiling and upbeat wherever you go.

When you and others you connect with feel good more people want to be your friends. People will fall in love with you more easily. Some people will offer you opportunities, jobs, adventures and all sorts of things just because you learned to control what you think and how you feel.

Soon, you'll take charge of your entire *destiny* through making this one tiny change on a consistent basis. You may or may not believe in the law of attraction, (I do, but it wasn't always thus), but it doesn't matter. *This works anyway.*

I've tried to steer a middle course between the ancient and modern metaphysical notions and the very modern quantum science that now, somewhat reluctantly it has to be said, has come to agree with what ancient civilizations have been saying for aeons.

You may have heard that to successfully bring your dreams into being you must be able to visualise. But for this "method" there is no requirement that you know how to visualise – you already know enough about how to *imagine* things!

Also, although I and with many other teachers of happiness-related topics, would recommend meditation as a daily practice, once again my own experience was that as I relaxed and found that life came more easily to me, I *naturally* wanted to deepen and prolong the experience – and so I was drawn to meditation. I have included some basic information about meditation later on – but please don't skip ahead. If and when you are ready to introduce meditation into your life, (if you haven't already), once again, it will feel effortless and natural.

Nothing will feel like an effort of will any more. Good things will happen to you all the time, as they do to me – and you will see and *appreciate* the good things you already have as they come more and more into the foreground of your awareness.

There is no reason why most things shouldn't go *right*. Most things do, after all! When was the last time your TV or even your astonishingly complex computer or phone didn't work at the flick of a switch? At what point in your life have you ever had to worry that a cut finger wouldn't heal? Or that the Earth would stop spinning?

These things – to name far less than the tip of the iceberg – are *miraculous* without having to stretch anyone's imagination, yet we take them for granted.

Look around you and you will see that life is working pretty well almost all the time. You may have just watched a news bulletin about a war somewhere but the very least you could do is get some perspective on that. How many countries right now are *not* at war?

I am not advocating a Pollyanna-ish mentality. But I am suggesting that we urgently need to get our heads out of the doom-mongering mentality that is the vogue at the moment.

*"I am old and I have had many troubles – most of which have never happened." – Old proverb.*

So as we set sail on our great voyage together I encourage you to think about that in the full and absolute knowledge that you *can*.

Change begins with you.

Let's be quite clear about that, even though you may not accept or believe that yet. *All* change begins – and ends - with you. If you want better health, more money, people to treat you better, new love in your life – whatever it is you want, that change will only come about when *you* change.

The techniques outlined in this book are designed to show you *how* to change. As always in life, you have a choice. You could choose to skip this chapter altogether.

You can resist the idea that all change begins and ends with you. You can continue blaming your past or your mother or the government or global warming or … whatever you like for the conditions of your life. You can continue to say that you "can't help it" – whatever "it" is.

All of these options will keep you stuck and you may as well give this book to someone who is serious about change right now if that's where you are in your head.

I'm beseeching you to *try* these things out. As you will hear me say elsewhere in this book, the worst that can happens is that you'll feel good more of the time, so it's hardly onerous!

Moreover, the techniques are simple, fast and fun to do. Approach them in the spirit of play and have fun as you test out what lies ahead. Lighten up!

## *What You Want*

Although everyone is a unique individual, as human beings we have some fundamentals in common. This is true irrespective of your culture, gender, age or any other variable. Perhaps the most fundamental of all is that when you want something – anything – to change, *the only change you ever want is a change in the way you feel.*

You may think that it is some circumstance or even other person, (boss, mother-in-law, spouse, teenager…) which is the cause of your all your troubles, but it remains true that what you need first, foremost and possibly last, is to *feel* better about things. Only then can further change take place.

Einstein himself is credited with coming up with this definition of insanity:

*…doing the same thing over and over again and expecting a different result.*

You are unlikely to resolve a relationship issue if you are angry. You are just as unlikely to make money if you persist in worrying about your lack of it. The fact is, you must learn to put yourself in a more resourceful state of mind before anything will change.

The principle then is: *feel better first.*

Most of us are conditioned to think that *when* things change *then* you'll feel better, but that is the tail wagging the dog!

The great news is that you are in charge of the way you feel, not your situation or other people.

Of course, when things are going well you generally don't ask for help. Nobody ever tries to reverse engineer their happiness whilst they're feeling good to see how to maintain it! That isn't a criticism; on the contrary, that is as it should be. It would be a sad old world indeed if we had to go navel gazing whenever we felt good just to try to stay feeling good. The result would be instantaneous loss of good feeling since it would dissolve into worry about worse times to come!

This state of affairs is a big clue that happiness is our natural state. Unhappiness of any kind is merely a warning that something is out of balance and all we need to do is to rebalance things and life will be tickety-boo once more.

Just as physical pain is a warning that something needs attention, so emotional discomfort functions in precisely the same way. Thus worries, fear, anxiety – along with all "negative" emotions – are perfectly natural and very useful. They are our signal that change is required.

They were never intended to be a permanent way of life. We are now living in times where we are fed things to worry about as a daily diet, so that even when our own lives are running smoothly there are any number of issues you could choose to focus upon that could scare the living daylights out of a saint, let alone the rest of us ordinary mortals.

Am I suggesting that we should all bury our heads in the proverbial sand and hope all the nightmares go away? Not at all. What I am saying is that I don't believe that any of us can hope to make one iota of difference to a single problem, personal or global, by being afraid or angry. Those emotions are futile as problem solvers, or, if given enough room to vent, they simply add more fuel to situations that are already inflamed.

For far too long, too many of us have accepted worry and stress and personal unhappiness of one kind or another as the norm. They are not only willing to go through life sick and tired, in every sense of both terms, but many bring up their children in that kind of negatively charged environment – however unwittingly. Even the most "well balanced" of families can thus produce children who are taking anti-depressants before they reach puberty! Fear and anxiety have become more common emotions than joy, playfulness, creativity and sheer love of life. It's become a cultural habit.

Things happen in anyone's lives that are beyond personal control. When I was seven I lost my five year old sister to a kidney complaint. Our mother, who never recovered from her grief, died just two years later, taken by breast cancer. She was forty.

Neither of these events was foreseeable or preventable as far as anyone can tell. The effects on me and the remnants of my family were, of course, immense but are not for documenting here, not because they are unimportant but because they are irrelevant. All, that is, save one.

The most potent and long lasting effect of the two deaths that occurred during my childhood that I am conscious of is that by the time I was thirteen I had decided in my young mind that any unhappy states within our family were understandable because of the tragedies we had endured. Other families, I naively reasoned, would therefore mostly be happy.

I determined, out of this logic, to hang out with friends whose families were whole.

The shock realisation, as you might imagine, however, was that other people mostly were not especially happy! Instead, they disliked their own bodies, they had relationship "problems," self esteem issues and money worries to name but a common few. In some cases they – or their parents – had troubled marriages, depression in the family and guilty secrets that kept them awake at night.

To me, this was absurd. We were – and still are - living in the most privileged time in history. Even the poorest of us probably has more choice of what to eat than all the kings and queens of history as just one example. Opportunities are boundless and free time for taking advantage of them is more available than to any previous generation.

People, in other words, were unhappy for no reason! At least, not that I could see.

Of course, this was a somewhat naïve viewpoint to say the least. In the four decades since my mother's passing I can hardly claim to have had an utterly trouble-free life. But my innocent teenage philosophy laid a foundation for my life that I shall be eternally grateful for. I have never lost the belief that happiness is available to us all, that it is our birthright, and no matter what happens, a choice we can make.

What follows in this book is to some extent the art of making conscious what seems instinctive. True instinct – such as the will to survive – is often confused with habitual responses, as in the case of addictions for example. No one is born with or would ever develop an "instinct" to inhale poisonous fumes – but smokers do it many times a day for decades, often until it kills them, as we know. That is by no means an instinct.

By the same token, whilst anger may have some legitimate instinctive basis as a useful survival tool, (it was probably handy to get riled at a wild beast attacking you or your family when we were cave dwellers), violence towards other people, or indeed other species, is not an instinctive response. Managing anger, or indeed any emotion is certainly highly achievable, and I don't subscribe to the "I can't help it" school of thought.

My most basic premise, then, is that we each have the capacity to choose how we live and how we are. It's called "response-ability" – the ability to respond *by choice* to life.

My other, equally basic premise is that happiness is our natural state. I firmly believe that we can all excel in life, live in full health, have joyful and meaningful relationships and passionately embrace every waking moment of our lives. And to add to that, we should all sleep well too!

We seem to arrive on this planet with our agenda already set to some degree. A person who loves to sing is not going to be happy being railroaded into a career as a surgeon, for example, even though from an outsider's perspective they might appear highly successful.

# 3: Two Fundamental Skills

Once you know how to take charge of that incredible device inside your skull you will forever more be empowered to choose the direction your life takes and your happiness and success are absolutely assured.

Really. That is a guarantee I can make to you unreservedly.

If you've ever changed your mind about anything – even as miniscule as "I used to take sugar in my tea but now I prefer it unsweetened," – you can do this. What it boils down to is changing your mind about yourself. Oh, and doing it in a way that you know you're doing it!

It's thinking and being with *awareness*. Human beings have the remarkable ability to do that, and it's not for nothing that we do!

## *Self Belief & Certainty*

You require just two skills to make it all happen. The first, and perhaps most important, is utter, unshakeable belief in yourself.

The second is having the certainty that no matter what happens you are in the driving seat, able to control the direction of your life.

Once you have these mastered, everything else in respect of mental troubles will be easy to fix without ever needing to resort to chemicals, electric shocks or psychiatric intervention.

I know that these are bold claims – or will seem so for many. I trained as a psychiatric nurse and I am well aware of how powerful a grip the model of orthodox psychiatric medicine has in our present culture. Perhaps I should state before proceeding further with this line of argument that I am not against modern psychiatric medicine – I have seen it help a great many people who might otherwise have remained incarcerated in institutions or at least very miserable for the rest of their lives without the intervention of psychiatry. Indeed, I'm not *against* anything. But I am definitely *for* self empowerment – which I believe can and perhaps should include healing of many kinds, from physical ailments to mental distress.

Furthermore, although this is a book about self help, I will state right here that sometimes one of the most courageous acts you can make in respect of helping yourself is actually admitting that there are times when you cannot continue alone and need to ask for, and accept, help from others. Psychiatric medicine may be the crutch you need to lean on for a while.

If I was opposed to psychiatry I would be claiming that I believe that it doesn't work, which is far from the case. However, it is frequently a hit and miss affair. You can't see someone's mental suffering or even measure it in the same way that you can heal, say, a broken bone. For the same reasons it is almost impossible to say when a mental condition is "fixed" or "cured."

Also, we need to define what we mean by something "working". Antibiotics "work" when we can see in a laboratory test that the invading bacteria have gone away. That's a measurable result.

But all too often the goal of psychiatry is a compromise. Some medicines can, it seems, dampen down negative or anxious feelings, but they do little if anything to change the fundamental nervous character of the person, who then becomes dependent on both the pills and the doctors in what is often a downward spiral of neediness for the rest of their lives.

Worse than even this, to my mind, is the underlying sense that is prized as well as taken almost for granted by our culture, that some outsider – the doctors – can be an expert on our individuality and know more about us than we ourselves do. General medicine too is built on this cornerstone belief.

I reiterate: I am not opposed to the medical model. But it is not the *only* model of healing. The danger is that we give up all responsibility, each of us individually that is, for every twinge, cough, splutter or behaviour and seek an "expert" opinion on whether we're still all right at every turn of life.

Also, a fundamental principle of the Western medical model is to wait until you're "broken" in some way, to then figure out just which part of you is broken, (called "diagnosis"), and then to "fix" you usually with powerful and dangerous chemicals.

You weren't born broken. Wholeness is your natural state. Indeed, the words "health" and "whole" and even "holy" come from the same root. Why should we even think that we can become broken?

## There's Nothing "Wrong" With You!

Now I know that you may be reading this from a sick bed, perhaps with a bevy of doctors and nurses scampering around in an attempt to "fix" you. For one moment, try a little experiment, would you? You're still included even if you're in perfect, robust health. Just think of a time when you've ever wondered what's wrong with yourself in any way at all – just a piece of behaviour, a "crazy" decision or an odd lapse of concentration will do.

Don't read further until you've got some reference for that state of mind.

Okay, now try this:

Think of a time when you were on a journey, maybe in a car, but a train or most land based journeys will be fine. (Planes are more difficult because you usually don't know where you are – geographically speaking – until you're almost landing).

Now, you're on a journey. You are going somewhere and you started from somewhere else, obviously! When you arrive you will have the sense of pleasure at having arrived safe and sound, and hopefully this is also a place you're looking forward to getting to. (If you picked a journey with a sense of dread about your arrival, choose a different one!)

Let us suppose you're about half way there. You look out of the window at whatever you can see. Some landmarks will help you to identify – at least roughly – where you are.

You're on your way. You're still travelling. You are neither at the start or end place, just travelling. Would you say, "What's *wrong* with this place? This isn't where I want to be?"

Of course you wouldn't! You are simply passing through. This is a place on your journey you happen to have noticed.

Now it may be that you have been forced to stop by something unforeseen. A traffic jam or even your own car breaking down. Do you remember such occasions? Almost certainly you do.

Are you still there? Are you out on the road somewhere in a traffic jam that's lasted perhaps ten years? Is your car still broken?

Of course it isn't! You got home somehow. The situation got resolved. Somebody may have helped you, especially if you called a breakdown service for example. Or maybe, if it was a traffic jam, eventually the traffic just moved again.

The curved balls life will sometimes throw our way don't mean there's anything *wrong*. Two plus two equals five is *wrong*, but you undergoing some change is just a place you're passing through, as is all of life.

I know it's "only" a figure of speech, but figures of speech reveal underlying beliefs and cultural attitudes. If you are sick, wouldn't it change the way you feel about your condition to some degree if you thought of it as a challenging time you're passing through, and to which you will eventually figure out a solution, rather than there being something wrong with you that you must battle against?

I've laboured this point for another reason too. This is a seed of discovering that you can shift your thought patterns and that by doing so you get a corresponding shift in your emotions. It's a tiny shift in this case, but as I'm sure you know, if a ship or plane's course is altered by even so much as a fraction of a degree, the result will be that, over the length of a long journey, it will arrive somewhere utterly different than if the adjustment had not been made.

These tiny shifts can change your *destiny*. They cost nothing and they take fractions of a second to do. You are flexing the mental muscle that was never trained at school – or indeed anywhere else in all probability. In fact, it's unlikely that anyone ever told you that you even have such a "muscle" - so exercising it will feel odd.

You'll notice resistance. Your "familiar" thought patterns will tell you that "it doesn't really work" or "this can't possibly make a difference" or something like that. That's fear, and that's okay. We're all conditioned to fear change, and the ego doesn't like having its cage rattled. It likes to tell you that "common sense" knows best.

Old patterns do take conscious application to break, but eventually they become the norm. If that wasn't true, you would never have learned to walk! As a human being you are a member of the most adaptable species that has ever lived. We can adapt to extreme climates, an enormous range of diets, environments of many kinds. You can most certainly adapt to the experience of consciously directing your mind to improve your life – the rewards are phenomenal, so there'll be no shortage of incentives!

I'm going to repeat what I said just a few paragraphs ago about your only needing two skills – that of unshakeable belief in yourself and total certainty that, no matter what happens you can reach your goal.

Why do I bother to repeat it? I assure you it isn't because I'm running short of ideas! The reason is far more important than that: the chances are that you don't really believe me.

You, in common with most of the rest of the human race, will have had experiences that have apparently taught you that reaching for the stars is for children and perhaps adolescents, but as a grown up you have to "get real" or "be realistic." Besides, you don't want to be disappointed do you? So play it safe!

Safety, I'm here to tell you, is also a state of mind! There is no such thing as a "safe" job or a place that can guarantee it will never have a natural disaster or that criminals never inhabit.

You get to feel safe when you trust in something bigger than both of us – but I'll leave that for a later chapter.

Sadly, a huge number of people go through life expecting things to go wrong and feeling that they personally could never amount to anything. Indeed, many folks feel it's been a struggle to get to wherever they are and just as much of one to stay there.

I say sadly because no child ever dreams of living on a minimum wage or less, or of driving a shabby old car, let alone of divorce, redundancy or any other condition that leads us to despair and hopelessness at worst and a general disappointment with life at best.

It just shouldn't be that way. And it needn't be.

Hopefully, now you can see why those two "skills" as I've called them are the most important you can cultivate and master if you are to help yourself out of any kind of troubled mind. Once you have a handle on them, you will feel empowered and in control.

I have heard the great self help teacher Dr. Wayne Dyer ask his audiences this question:

*"If I have two wands, let's call one "A" and the other "B" and you can choose which one of them I wave, but you can only have one. Each wand can only be waved once.*

*W and A will give you anything you desire – a luxury car, millions in the bank, a new home – anything. And wand B will give you inner peace for the rest of your life no matter what shows up. Which will you choose?"*

It's a great question! I hope there is no doubt in your mind as to your answer.

Let us, then, set about installing these two great skills. Each will take you a little practice, that is you will need to consciously remind yourself to follow a few simple instructions on a regular basis for a short while – a few weeks is usually ample. You will discover that, despite the simplicity of the processes and the tiny amount of time you need to invest, you will meet resistance within yourself.

I've touched on this once already, and I will mention it again throughout this book because it's a major stumbling block – unless you're aware of it. Once you know what to look out for and how to deal with it, it's a pussy cat!

Your ego gets scared – it's like a frightened toddler. It doesn't want you to change things. It can't see that it will improve its life because it fears that it will have no role. After all, it has spent its time telling you to "be careful" and filling your head with other advice gleaned from perhaps your mother, grandparents, father, teachers or even your mates that all made sense at the time.

To assuage it, all you need do is talk to it like a caring but firm parent, and get on with the project – that of changing your life for the better forever – regardless. Therefore, all you need to be able to do is to recognise its voice.

Your ego, you see, thinks it *is* you. It thinks it's your identity, when in fact it is no more *you* than your body is *you*. You live within a body, but you will have noticed that that body changes dramatically without *you* doing a thing!

You may say, "I just woke up in a bad mood today," or "the traffic jam on my commute to work really stressed me," but those are nothing more than conditioned responses. I know people who use traffic jams to take little mini meditation breaks and arrive at their destination serene and smiling! After all, you won't change the traffic jam by raging at it, so make a different choice about how you react and watch your life change!

This should be very liberating, but I know it can also be scary too. It's liberating because you finally get to realise that you *are* in control. No one else can put you in a bad mood unless you choose to buy into their misery or accept their insults. No circumstance can faze you as long as you know that you have within you the resources to turn it around – which you always do as long as you're breathing and conscious.

The scariness comes from the naked feeling that you can't blame anyone or anything any more. All your excuses for why your life isn't working in some area or other are stripped away. For a lot of people this is too much and they prefer the relative misery and so-called safety of not changing and still being able to blame anyone and everything for their plight.

So, like everything else in this world, self reliance is double edged. If you think that you'll miss being able to blame your mother, mother-in-law, circumstance of birth, abusive childhood or you-fill-in-the-blank for your lack of happiness or achievement, then frankly you have already abandoned hope.

You can now add to your list that the advice in this book is no good and use it as a doorstop if you so desire.

I know I'm being harsh. One of my early teachers of psychotherapy taught me that a good therapist supports with one hand whilst slapping the client across the face with the other! That was, I know, a bit of a slap in the face. I apologise for the stinging sensation but if it has made you sit up ready to read the next and most important section it was worth it, so I hope you can forgive me.

Change is not difficult. But the *idea* of change can be scary. It's getting you past that that is the major achievement. Once you've done that you're as good as home and dry! *Why,* though, is change frightening? After all, it's what you seem to want – until it actually looks possible!

## *Why People Resist Change.*

People always do things for a reason, and that reason will always be to move themselves in one of two directions, namely, towards some pleasure (or anticipated pleasure), or away from some pain, including emotional pain, or anticipated pain. The emotional variety of anticipated pain is called *fear.*

You can get a lot of payoffs from having problems. One of the biggest is often simply the need to be liked. Moaners and complainers are everywhere – it's easy to belong to that club! It can even be competitive. We've all heard people say, on hearing someone's troubles, "Just *wait* 'til I tell you what happened to *me!*" As if having a more magnificent problem was some kind of trophy! But if your problems go away, won't you also lose your friends?

Of course in reality that isn't what happens! Some friends you have already will follow your example and others will fall away and find new companions to moan about life with. But you will gain new, more successful friends as you become happier and more successful in your life – people who share those values. Some will become mentors and teachers too. You will certainly never be alone! Nevertheless, in the beginning, trusting that you can not only leave the "rock bottom club" but also that there will still be people out there who will like you even more once you do is not easy.

Fear not. I'm here to hold your hand as well as show you the ladder out of the hole!

Another huge – and equally unconscious – payoff for keeping your problems is that it gives you significance. Telling people you have an unusual problem keeps their interest although what is overlooked is that it also keeps you as well as them in the mire. Everyone shaking their heads and saying, "Tut, tut! Isn't it awful?" is hardly a formula for success and happiness!

These issues boil down to fear of abandonment or of not being loved, which is the same thing really. It's fundamental to all human beings – we're wired to need love. Our very survival depends on it from the moment we emerge from the womb – literally. If a baby's cry did not result in being both fed and held it would soon fail to thrive and before very long, die.

Is there an antidote then? Since this is part of our very psychological make up it might at first seem that you are powerless to do anything about reactions like these, and that would mean you're stuck with your problems!

Fortunately there is a simple solution. Simple, but that word isn't synonymous with "instant" and for some, not with "easy" either. Once again you will need to become your own monitor, watching your own reactions, but you *can* do it. You have this ability too, so exercise it!

As with all the processes and ideas for change I'll outline in this book, you have to think of them like a toddler learning to walk. You are discovering and exercising muscles that you've probably never used before. But quitting is not an option. If it was, most of us would still be crawling around on the floor!

If you stumble or can't quite make it to where you thought you'd get to, have a *little* rest, then pick yourself up and do it again – as many times as it takes to get to where you want to go, and beyond.

Think of the world of unforeseen opportunities open up to a child once it can walk! When it first tries to walk its goal is only to take a step or two. I doubt it ever considers that it will be able to get into cupboards or other previously unexplored places. It almost certainly doesn't think that soon, even if Mummy is a hundred metres away it can still run to her and will no longer need to rely on her approach to reach her – and so on.

You can have no idea of the millions of opportunities you will open up for yourself now as an adult by making even a tiny change to the way you handle your life.

The first part of the "antidote" to holding onto problem and unwanted patterns of behaviour then, is to become aware of them.

The second element is to remind yourself as often as necessary of the freedom and rewards that await you as you make these changes.

Remember I told you that we are all motivated to move towards pleasure, or anticipated pleasure, and away from pain or anticipated pain? Well, there is your reminder of pleasure!

You can strengthen that pull too, as I will show you later.

But for now, remember that there are two ends to that spectrum. If you find you can't muster the motivation to change one day, flip to the other end of the spectrum by asking yourself one simple question:

*What will my life be like if I don't change right now?*

Ask yourself what it will be like in a month, a year, ten years time. Consider all the elements of your life. What will have happened to your career, your relationships, your health or your finances if you don't change *now?*

I'm going to offer you one more "tool" too that I will use in many contexts because this is extraordinarily adaptable, useful and important. It's simply this: **remember that for change to be effective it doesn't have to be dramatic!**

It *could* be dramatic and massive but that isn't required. A *tiny* change will do – for now at least. Changing from a negative feeling such as worry or stress, for example, can be eradicated with nothing more than a couple of deep breaths! Oh, sure, you'll probably start worrying again within the next sixty seconds, but that time can also be enough to have a flash of inspiration – or simply to "get" the message that worry isn't going to solve the problem anyway!

Look, although it won't remove most problems or limiting behaviours, the very fact that you've started to *think* about making changes means you're on your way. You should be patting yourself on the back for that alone.

As a matter of fact, that's a very important point right there. I've led dozens of workshops where if I've so much as hinted that I'm going to suggest that participants look at loving themselves, they will begin protesting! Really! Think what that means!

Here we are, wanting to be liked, accepted and loved for who we are, and we can't love ourselves! If you saw a great movie that deeply moved you, you'd tell everyone about it wouldn't you? You'd tell them how much you loved it, and you would do so with a great deal of passion and enthusiasm. You might, as a result, send several people to see it. This is how word of mouth spreads, of course.

And yet, if you had to tell someone about yourself, at an interview or on a *date* for heavens' sake, unless you're a rare individual, you'll be half hearted at best, coy, shy and unassuming. You will, in all probability, do your utmost to convince the other person that you are for the most part, ordinary, with just one or two mildly interesting characteristics that may make you worthy of a second glance.

Oh boy!

This is a theme I'll return to later in this book, but for now let me take the anxiety out of it for you. Please understand that at no point will I be suggesting that you arrogantly puff yourself up and brag about how great you are. True greatness never comes that way in any case! (It would be bestowed upon you by others for one thing – it's something you earn, like respect).

What I am suggesting, for now at least, is that you simply *acknowledge* your achievements, strengths and talents – the ones you've acquired or mastered so far in your life – and that from this day forward you *catch yourself in the act of doing something good, no matter how small.*

Consciously acknowledge your progress. I say again, this does not have to involve grand, dramatic, sweeping changes. "A journey of a thousand miles begins with a single step" Lao-Tsu taught us two and a half thousand years ago, and his wisdom is profoundly true today as it will always be. A thought of wanting to change is a single step.

That thousand mile journey would then continue with a second step, so if and when you take that one, acknowledge yourself for that too. What might that be? In some way, it would mean acting on that first thought. That may be reading a chapter, (a page ... a paragraph?), of this book. Or it may be remembering to smile at your grumpy neighbour in the morning.

*Small steps are okay. As long as you keep taking them, you will complete your thousand mile journey!*

And if you rest a while, don't beat yourself up with guilt. Simply acknowledge that that is what you need to do right now and allow your rest to be, well, restful.

And if you find yourself returning to some of your old ways, (e.g. putting weight on that you'd lost, slipping back into an addiction, or maybe just not cleaning out those cupboards until you can't see the "use by" dates), again don't beat yourself up. Hardly anyone – perhaps nobody – goes from negative old pattern to positive new pattern in one straight, continuous line of progress.

Besides, life happens and gets in the way. Just when you thought you were getting somewhere, there's a shake-up at work and you're redundant, or your teenager gets into trouble or your pet dies … things happen that you can't foresee in everyone's life, and it can knock the best of us off balance for a while.

Whilst none of us can have the crystal ball that would be required to predict all of it, you can be better prepared for all the curved balls life can throw your way by having a steady state of inner peace. Does this mean you will never get upset or be ruffled by anything ever again?

Of course not! You'd need to be a robot for that to be the case. But it does mean that you're equipped for an emotional storm and that you will return to an even keel very quickly.

The older you get the more important this becomes too. When you're in your twenties, thirties or even forties perhaps, it's not so terrible if you take ten years to recover from say a major heartbreak or some other life changing event. But you can't afford the "luxury" of a decade of recovery every time something happens that you didn't plan for! You'll only get a handful of goes at that! So it's vitally important that you learn skills that can get you to the other side of life's challenges quickly.

"Skill" is perhaps not the right word. It is not a technique; it's a way of life. You need a philosophy that makes sense to you and that works in all situations. I'm going to give you that – or at any rate I'll show you how to find your own! As you work through the sections of this book, you will find all you need to give yourself the complete toolkit required to fix, understand and recover from any problem life throws at you – whether in your external circumstances or your emotional or spiritual condition. As a result, you will also be able to keep yourself in better physical shape too, as well as having a deep wellspring of resources to handle the emotional fallout that can result from complex or dangerous physical diagnoses.

In short, there'll be nothing you can't handle!

# 4: Who You Really Are –
# (And Why You're Here)

If you're going to have belief in yourself then you'd better know precisely who and what your "self" is! In this short chapter I'll lead you through a train of thought that will open up possibilities about who you are and where you belong in the "grand scheme" of things! Then we'll explore why you're here!

This is a real "building block" chapter – so don't skip it!

To begin, take a moment to recall the last time you were introduced to someone for the first time. How did the conversation go? Something like this perhaps:

"Joe, this is Jane.

"Hi Jane," (shaking hands).

"Hi Joe. What do you do?"

"Oh, I _____," (you fill in the blank with your occupation here). "What about you?"

Jane proceeds to name her job.

If you are both willing to get a little better acquainted, you might ask about children and one or two other minor details that are considered socially acceptable and polite.

At the end of it, you will have gleaned a tiny number of facts about Jane, and she about you. (I've called you Joe for this example. Live with it!) But that isn't really what's important to either of you, although it may prove useful should you meet again.

What's really important is whether you both *enjoyed* the experience of meeting one another. You knew in the first couple of nano-seconds if you liked each other. Both of you will have sized that up.

Now, I want you to reconsider the question of who you actually are. Here's a question for you to ask yourself: Have you ever thought, felt or said, "I *am* my body?"

I'd be very surprised if you answered in any language anything other than, "No. Of course not!"

You see, Jane could see your body, but that isn't you. You would never say, "I am my body," in any circumstances. You have a sense of *having* one, but it isn't *you* per se. Besides, it changes all the time. The body that you had when you were three months old, for example, not only doesn't look anything like you now, but it literally no longer exists. There isn't one cell or molecule of it here today. It isn't dead, but it isn't in the physical realm any more either.

In fact, the body that you had just seven years ago has been *completely replaced*. All thirteen trillion cells of it. And in seven years time, the body that you inhabit now will have gone too.

Your body changes shape, changes colour, bits fall off or out, markings and blemishes appear and disappear and so on. Most of this is as much of a surprise to you as it is to anyone else.

Nope. Your body isn't you.

So how about your personality? Surely *that's* you, isn't it? People would describe you by it. "Oh, Joe's got such a lovely sense of humour." Hmm. You may *have* a sense of humour, but once again, this is something you have, like a possession. But no one would say, "Joe *is* a sense of humour." You may possess many other qualities. Perhaps you're intelligent, sporty, academic, deep thinking ... you name it. Those are still attributes you *have*, they aren't you. And, like your body, your personality can also change, along with your values and beliefs for example.

So you're not your personality. That's something else you *have*, but it isn't you.

How about your thoughts? Are they you, or do you *have* thoughts?

Let me just ask you that question again, only this time I want you to notice the subtle shift in emphasis.

How about your thoughts? Are they you, or do *you* have thoughts? (Just who is it exactly that *has* the thoughts, the personality, the body ...?)

What about your feelings? Surely *they* are what you are? But no, a quick examination of personal experience will once again reveal that there's a *you* who *has* emotions, but no one ever says "I am my feelings."

By now, you will be starting to see that you are not your physical self and you aren't your experiences either. So what in heaven's name does that make you?

After all, you can change your mind, (i.e. your thoughts), and you can change your view or opinion of something which is to say you can feel differently about it. Your body changes too, much of it without your conscious interference it's true, but you also exert some influence over that too. More than you probably realise – we'll look at that topic in more depth later on.

*"You"* then, are *aware* of having a body, thoughts, feelings, opinions, hopes, ambitions and so on, but none of them are not you. You are that *pure awareness* at the centre of all the action.

Awareness. That's what you are. Consciousness mixed with intelligence if you want to put it in simpler language. Some people have referred to this as "the witness", others have called it "your inner being" but it really doesn't matter what you call it. As you will have seen, it's easier to define what it *isn't*.

That's because it has no form or boundaries of any kind.

That means it has no beginning or end, because things that aren't physical aren't bound by physical laws are they? That's knocked death on the head then!

For now, that will do. I've made you aware that you are awareness. You may or may not have a strong sense of that at this point, but not to worry. As you work through this book you will come to *experience* it – then you'll know for yourself.

Having established *what* you are, we are still left with a much more important question. At least it is for most people. That question is:

## *"Why Am I Here?"*

Let's make an assumption, shall we? Call it a hypothesis if you like. Hypotheses are used by scientists and other researchers as a working theory that can be tested. If it fails it can be abandoned and another hypothesis is sought. If it holds up under scrutiny and repeated testing it is said to be proof and science is advanced by one more step.

Now, I can't offer you scientific proof of the hypothesis I'm going to put forward in a moment because this isn't provable, at least not at our present level of understanding. You will have to judge for yourself if it feels right or not, but we can put it under a bit of scrutiny.

Here's my hypothesis: **You are here because you _want_ to be.**

Now that presupposes that you had some kind of sentient existence before you were born and a lot of other things besides.

To see if the hypothesis has legs, let's consider one of the most popular alternatives which would be that you're here by some accident of birth. Now, I can go along with the notion that your parents did what they did – under whatever circumstances – to create a baby which then turned out to be you.

According to the "accident of birth" model, you have to take on board everything about yourself and say it was all chance. That means all your hopes, dreams, ideas and foibles. It means taking into account this particular time and culture and everything you have at your disposal. (I'm typing this on a computer that I understand has many times more capacity than the ones that sent man to the Moon. And mine was a darned site cheaper too!)

I mean, could you have been _you_ if you had been born five hundred years ago? Or on a different continent? And then there's the old conundrum about who you might have been if another sperm had won the race to your mother's ovary!

We take the everyday for granted but in fact it's miraculous. We know precisely what elements make life but we can't make it ourselves. I've mentioned elsewhere that all the elements contained in a bicycle frame are present in the gases and lava spewed out by volcanoes, but in all the millennia of spewing not one volcano has produced so much as a single spoke, let alone a bike!

Life is *not* random. I'm sorry, but there's too much order for there to be chaos.

I realise we're getting deep and philosophical here, but don't panic: you aren't required to know the answers. (I don't). I just want to "wake you up" enough for a moment so that you take a step back and instead of blindly accepting that everything is the way you've always seen it or been told that it is, ask yourself if that view really hangs together for you.

Let us now re-examine our working hypothesis. If you're here because you want to be then it follows that you would have chosen for yourself a life that feels good to you, wouldn't it?

Now, we need to be careful here. I wouldn't choose, from my perspective here on Earth, a childhood where my mother will die when I am nine years old. What child would choose that?

But suppose that wasn't what the choices were like. What if my agenda had been, "I want to teach emotional and spiritual health and self empowerment." As things have turned out I not only have travelled that path, but I was also born to parents with highly inquiring minds. And furthermore I have grown up in an age where mass communication has never been easier, faster or cheaper.

Could I have fulfilled that agenda if I had been born, say, into the Royal family? Or in a mud hut in Africa? Or five hundred years ago?

It's possible, of course, in any scenario. But what I know is that I love who I am and how my life – and my personality – has turned out. I feel fulfilled and joyful and grateful for my life every day. Would I have wanted my mother to die? Of course not! I'm not saying that. This is 20/20 hindsight.

Nor am I saying that to have a fulfilled life you have to suffer first.

What I am saying, however, is that *if* you suffer and *when* you feel bad, sad or mad at life you *also* need to know that these are lessons you have the resources within you to turn around. They are powerful pointers that throw into sharp relief what you really want from life because you know you would never desire anything so painful.

The key word here is "contrast" and I am grateful to the teacher Abraham-Hicks for pointing it out more powerfully than anyone else I know.

Some people seem to know much earlier in life than I did what their agenda is. Jamie Cullum was virtually established as a "jazz great" by the time he was twenty one, for example. It is clear, at least to me – and I should have thought to practically everyone – that he is born to play music. One can hardly imagine him spending the first twenty years of his life as a lawyer or anything else!

Whatever age you are, and regardless of what you have already been through or not been through, somewhere inside you there is a dream.  You may need to wake it up again, or you may need to waken it for the very first time, but I know you sense that I am right.  Or you may already know what it is.

It will be a yearning, burning inside you.  It will have a purpose and it will be something that makes a difference.  (Music makes people feel good).  I always wanted to write books and teach self empowerment.

Here are a few characteristics I had as a child that now make this obvious:

- I loved writing essays at school.  If we had an essay set as homework I would silently cheer.  All the other boys hated them.
- I came top in English at school year after year.
- When my mother would explain an adult story to me, (like a book or a film we'd seen on TV), I would stand in front of a mirror explaining it back to an imaginary audience.  I was perhaps five or six years old.
- As a teenager, I read psychology books for "fun."
- I studied Zen at the age of seventeen because it taught effortlessness.

And so on.

No one would choose homelessness, drug addiction, disease or pain as a lifestyle.  No one would deliberately design a life where they had to do a job they hate for forty years or to live with someone they don't love either, but millions of people do those things, *believing there is no real choice.*  It is that "stuck-ness" that I want to un-stick.  You *always* have a choice.

You came here to feel fulfilled – and what fulfils you probably won't do for me.  One of my old school friends, whom I still know forty years on, has always loved engineering feats.  He has built himself a working steam train and a full size steam boat in his time amongst other huge projects. I love the results, but I could hardly be less interested in the actual *doing* of such things.

Or to put it another way: your purpose in life is to be happy. That's it – that's your *only* purpose. Every one of us will have a different way for that happiness to be expressed, but there really is nothing else and no other point to life.

Your agenda is exclusively yours, but I know from the bottom of my heart that it was not to live frustrated and believing that life is just one long string of bill-paying and drudgery only to bring up the next generation to do the same! Life is meant to be joyful – your life and everyone's life. That is something we can both have and give to others by becoming an example and maybe by teaching it too.

Many have (almost) given up on that.

But you haven't, because if you had given up, you wouldn't be reading this.

There *is* a different way.

It's a way of being – and you're learning it now.

# 5: Decisions – The Foundation Of Certainty

The following story is probably apocryphal; I can't remember where I first heard it, but regardless of whether or not it has any basis in fact, its message is profound and important.

*It seems there was a CEO of a very successful multi-national corporation who was on the verge of retirement. His name was synonymous with the success of the company, and his imminent departure was seen with some trepidation by the board of directors and shareholders alike.*

*The CEO himself, however, was relatively unperturbed. He had carefully selected his successor, a young man who had all the attributes and qualities needed to carry the company forward and to develop it even further. The young man was a visionary who already had a formidable track record of his own. The CEO had no doubt that he had the right man for the job.*

*For the last few months of the elder gentleman's tenure, the younger man shadowed him, attending every meeting together, meeting the workforce, examining production lines and learning how the eagle-eyed CEO looked continually for ways to improve quality, productivity and good customer relations. He seemed to achieve all of these with ease.*

*Eventually, it came to the last week of the outgoing CEO's time with the company. And then, all too quickly, Monday rolled around into Friday.*

*The two men sat alone together facing each other across the polished mahogany desk.*

*"Well," the older man began, "on Monday morning this empire will all be yours and I shall be on the golf course. I am perfectly content with both of those notions. You are more than ready to take the reins, young man. Is there anything at all you'd like to ask me before I hand you the keys to the kingdom at five o'clock this afternoon?"*

*The young man thought for just a brief moment. "Sir," he said, "you have taught me well and I know I have skills of my own, but there is one thing that still bothers me."*

*"Ask away," said the elder, opening his palms. "Anything at all."*

*"Well," said the younger man, "you have a formidable reputation sir for being brilliant at making snap decisions and for always getting them right. How do you do that?"*

*The retiring CEO chuckled. "Yes, I have heard that said about me. But the reason I'm laughing is because you've rumbled my biggest secret. Let me tell you how I do that."*

*The younger man leaned forward on the edge of his seat.*

*"At home," the CEO began, "my wife keeps jars of dried beans in our kitchen, which also happens to be where I eat my breakfast." He paused to sip some water.*

*"When I finish my breakfast, as I leave the kitchen to go and get my hat and coat, I pass those jars of beans and I put my hand in and grab a handful of beans which I put in my left trouser pocket."*

*This was hardly what the young man had expected to hear and he was by now utterly transfixed by this strange story.*

*The older man continued, "Now you may have noticed that throughout my working day, questions get fired at me from all directions. My phone will ring, people will knock at my office door, and even over coffee someone can ask me a random question.*

*"Sometimes I have to decide how to deal with a takeover bid, or whether we should be trying one ourselves. Or perhaps I am required to decide whether to take on a new product or service, or whether to discontinue one that we've run for years. I have to make decisions regarding hiring and firing and all sorts of other issues that may pass across my desk.*

*"Of course, many of these things I can delegate these days, but even then I may be required to decide just whom I should delegate to."*

*The younger man was nodding fervently, still confused.*

*"Now," the elder went on, "if you have been very observant you will have noticed that whenever I am asked to make a big decision I have a habit of putting my left hand in my trouser pocket. That leaves my right hand free to speak on the phone or to pick up a pen and make notes."*

*"Yes," the younger man said, "I have seen you do that but I never thought anything of it."*

*"Of course not!" the older man chuckled. "But here is the secret. What I do is to grab a small handful of those dried beans in my pocket, and surreptitiously I count them out. And if the number is even, I agree to the decision, and if it is odd I oppose it. It's as simple as that."*

*The young man sat with his jaw wide open for what seemed like several minutes. Eventually, he managed to stammer, "B-but how can you make the right decision so often that way?"*

*Now it was the older man's turn to lean forward in his chair. "That is where the real secret lies," he half whispered. "People have the impression that I make the right decision more often than not, but I learned a very important truth early in my career."*

*"What is it?" the young man begged to know.*

*"It is far more important, in the eyes of other people, that you make some decision quickly rather than none or that you waver. If you procrastinate or change your mind, people lose confidence in you. And you lose it in yourself too. It's the certainty they want.*

*"Each decision I make has consequences and leads to a series of further sub-decisions, any of which can be handled by my counting beans method. I am not always right — in the sense that some people are always displeased whatever I decide — but I am always decisive. And that's what they like and respect. Anyone who comes to me with a "what shall we do?" question knows they will go away only moments later with an answer.*

*"And **that**," he concluded with an emphatic thump of his fist on his magnificent desk, "is how I built my reputation."*

Life is, it could be said, a series of decisions. You have to decide when it's safe to cross a road; your life depends on you being able to do that accurately every single time. And yet for most of us we wouldn't even consider that a difficult one! There are plenty more life changing decisions, from whether to marry, (or divorce), to have or not have kids, career choices, decisions about making a home and what kind of lifestyle suits you … the list is endless.

The better you are at making decisions, in general the more smoothly your life will flow. If you don't make decisions, you'll indulge in the opposite behaviour of procrastinating which is an utter waste of everyone's time, especially yours!

I'm going to say a few words here about time because I recognise that not everyone may see it in quite the way I do. Things, including money, to my way of thinking, are far less relevant to the quality of your life than time.

Let me explain what I mean by that. No matter which way you turn it, you cannot have today again. There are arguments for and against the existence of reincarnation, but to my knowledge not even the most devout believer has ever said, "Oh, it doesn't matter that I missed that opportunity; I can always do it again in my next lifetime."

This means that not only you, but the people – and indeed animals and possibly even plants – that you love will not be around forever. And neither will you. My contention is that you can always find a way to generate new money, (you'll have a lot more confidence about your resourcefulness by the time you've worked your way through this book), but you cannot generate new time. However, you can get more fulfilling and more frequently successful results *from* your time if you make good decisions.

The only question is, how do you know what constitutes a good decision?

Your life is about experiences. What you'll remember will be moments of love, of growth, of joy and yes, you will also recall the sad and the bad experiences, but I've already included them in my list. They're the moments of growth.

You won't get through life unscathed. If you're constantly trying to live a life free from disappointment, heartbreak or fear of any kind, you'll end up paralysed. That is what causes people to procrastinate – worrying and fretting that perhaps they'll have an experience that will be uncomfortable if they decide on X instead of Y, so they choose to decide on neither and hope the problem will go away. (This is, in effect, deciding not to decide, so you can't actually get away from decisions or from having to make them!)

Let me illustrate this by telling you another story, one which I know to be true because I was there.

Years ago, a friend of mine whom I'll call Bill, lived with his girlfriend in a house near the hospital where we both worked. Bill was then a nurse teacher, and as well as being a great friend, I also regard him as one of my mentors because he has innate wisdom – and wit – from which I have personally learned many valuable lessons.

Bill and Sal's house was a warm, welcoming place and all of their friends knew that anyone was welcome to drop in for coffee without pre-arrangement. On this cold December day, five or six of us had gathered after work and the conversation had turned to our respective Christmas plans. Finally someone asked Bill, who had been silent on this subject up to this point, what he would be doing on Christmas day.

Bill shuffled in his seat and looked momentarily uncomfortable, which was not typical. Clearing his throat, he announced, "I've decided not to have Christmas."

Of course we were confused and so we asked him what he meant.

He explained: "Well, I don't believe in the religious part of it. I have my own beliefs about God, but they aren't traditional Christian ones. And I don't choose to take a holiday in the middle of winter; I'd rather wait until spring. And I don't want people to give me gifts out of a sense of obligation. I'm very happy to give and receive gifts out of love or appreciation, but not because there's a date on the calendar and people feel under pressure to do it."

It was a powerful and impassioned speech. Sal, his girlfriend, was clearly nonplussed by the announcement; they'd obviously already discussed the issue. She, it transpired, would be spending her Christmas with her parents, and Bill would be alone in his house apart from their dog.

One friend, Liz, simply couldn't take it in. "What will you have for your lunch?" she asked, somewhat horrified.

Bill shrugged. "I dunno. Whatever's in the house. It'll just be a day off for me. Maybe beans on toast."

This was too much for Liz, who lived only a few doors away. "You're welcome to come to us. We'll have plenty of food." She was almost begging, desperate.

"Liz," said Bill patiently, "I don't think you've been listening to me. I'm not having Christmas - and you will be. It's a very kind thought, but I'll be fine here by myself thank you."

Liz processed this shocking idea for a moment longer, and as the penny dropped she blurted, "But won't you be lonely?"

Bill pondered before replying, "Well, I suppose I might be. And if I am, that'll be very interesting *because I haven't been lonely for years!*"

The point of telling that tale here is to illustrate that making a decision *in order* to avoid the possibility of an uncomfortable emotion may lead to your being inauthentic. Bill at least got to try out what it felt like to spend December 25th that year as if it was any other day. (I never found out whether he felt lonely or not).

Bill has since returned to having more traditional Christmases, but he has no regrets about that year. It felt right to him at the time and he learned many lessons about himself by allowing himself to follow his own path.

People will all too often avoid decisions, or choose the "safe" option, in case they make a "mistake." Yet, if you think about it, a "mistake" is rarely anything other than an undesirable or unpredictable outcome. Granted, if it's life or death you can't go back and do it again, but as I've already pointed out, merely crossing a road has that kind of weightiness, not to mention driving a car!

In many cases – perhaps even a majority – the "mistake" people fear the most is that someone else will disapprove! Someone might. So what? Did you expect everyone you ever meet to always like you until death do you part, amen? In my experience, the most popular and the easiest to love people are those who are authentic and live from their hearts.

I'm not encouraging you to take risks for the sake of it either! I am only pointing out that avoiding what could be an exciting and/or life changing option on the basis that it might not turn out as you hoped is not a reason not to do it.

All you'll get is a *result* – and you'll both be encouraged and empowered if you succeed, or you'll grow if it turns out to be another learning experience. Failure is not an option *because failure doesn't exist as long as you're moving forward and making decisions and choices in your life.*

Failure is when you realise your life is stale or stagnant and you *still* don't change!

Decisions *are* your life – a series of them one after the other. If you don't make them, someone else will make them for you. Other people will decide what kind of work you should do, when you should do it, when you can stop doing it and even what you should wear whilst you do it!

They'll tell you what to eat, what's good for you and what isn't, supposedly. People will instruct you and tell you how healthy you aren't, and what you should do to get in the kind of shape *they* think you should be in!

If you don't take charge, you'll find other people trying to tell you whom you should marry, when you should have kids and once you do, how you should bring them up! (To be just like *them* of course!)

On and on it goes, one "should" after another, brainwashing from advertising and the media. Watch and listen and pretty soon you'll "know" exactly what to be scared of and what opinions you "should" hold about people from other countries or with different cultural or religious beliefs to your own. There's always someone or some nationality to be scared of – but keep your wits about you because who it is can change without notice! Once it was the Germans, then it was the Russians, then Communists, (but China is a big commercial player these days so they're okay now), or it may be huge amorphous groups with names like Taliban or Al Qaeda.

When election time comes around, you can be fooled into believing that you are being given a free choice about who and what you are voting for, (although they'll try to convince you that it isn't really cool to opt out of voting entirely), but a little digging soon reveals that the people and organisations behind the public figures trying to win you over are in fact nothing like the faces you see every day on your TV and in the papers or on the internet. Sometimes they are food companies or oil giants or some such monster with a completely different agenda from the one you thought you were rooting for. (McDonalds was a major sponsor of Richard Nixon's presidential campaign, for instance).

You won't escape all of this, and I'm not suggesting you should even try to. You'd end up paranoid and exhausted. But I want you to really *get* that the more you know how to operate your own mind and the better your understanding of how the human mind works, (and there are human minds behind all of those corporations too, of course), the better chance you have of making a free or freer choice and also of seeing when and how manipulation is being worked on you!

There is some manipulation I don't mind too much, personally. I don't mind when a trailer "sells" me a really good movie. Or when some advertising lets me know of a really good book or about a new musical artiste I haven't discovered.

I don't mind, and a lot of the time I recognise at another level that I am being manipulated. I can really admire a well written advertisement or clever sales letter as a work of art. I suspect that there are times when I still don't catch on. But mostly I have a sense that I'm in charge of what I decide and what my tastes are.

The word "decision" literally means "to cut off from." Whereas "incision" is to cut into, de-cision is cutting of from all other possibilities. A decision is therefore not a wishy-washy half-hearted affair; it is certain, clear action. It is *commitment.*

## *Snap to it!*

Just like the story of the CEO and the beans at the beginning of this chapter, the secret to good decision making is often nothing more than the act of being decisive itself. It makes you feel strong and it gives others around you confidence in your confidence!

Wherever possible, don't dither or procrastinate. Make it your rule of thumb that you will make a decision in no more than sixty seconds. You can practice this with mail and emails that come your way. Do you need this message, yes or no? Quick! What's the answer?

Have your waste bin and shredder handy, and your finger hovering over the "delete" key on your computer. You'll be amazed at how much clutter you get rid of, and how much clearer your desk – and your mind – remain once you start this practice.

There are an amazing number of decisions that you can use this technique on. Where should you go on holiday this year? Are you going to go for that promotion this time around – yes or no?

## *The Intuitive Coin Toss Method*

You can even use a coin toss – but with a twist. If you're still uncertain after sixty seconds and you have an "A" or "B" decision to make, pull out a coin and assign option A to heads and B to tails. Spin the coin *and note your immediate reaction when it lands.*

If you have multiple choices, try dividing your options into two groups somehow, and then divide the chosen "winning" group – (using the intuitive method I'm about to describe below), and so on.

If you feel relief or pleased in some way, then go with that option. But if there's a pang of disappointment then you know that the *other* option is the one you should choose.

We are drifting into the realms of trusting your heart and your intuition here, and I will be saying a lot more about that in many other areas of this book, so this is a good practice run for you on that score too.

The trick is to go with your first reaction without giving yourself time to think about it. This is excellent practice for self awareness skills you'll be sharpening up later.

## *There __Is__ An Alternative!*

You don't have to make decisions of course. There are plenty of others willing to jump into the breach and make them for you.

Advertisers will tell you everything from what fashion to wear to what snack to put in your lunch box tomorrow.

The media will tell you what to think and what to be scared of. The education system will inform you as to what you should know and ignore the rest. Preachers will tell you what to believe in. And your boss will tell you what to do, when to do it, how long you can take over it, and even what to wear whilst you do it. (Your boss may also be someone you're married to!)

If you manage to avoid even all of these, nature itself will take over. That is human nature as well as Mother Nature. You will age and things around you will decay; that's Mother Nature. Human nature will incline towards giving up on you the more you choose to not change or procrastinate, so ultimately, taken to its extreme, you would end up lonely, old and friendless. And pretty ill.

"Habits rule the unreflecting herd" said Wordsworth. He was eloquently pointing out that if you don't think, (i.e. reflect), you will simply follow the majority. Is that so bad?

Well, no, not always it isn't. You can go too far the other way as well, of course. As a teenager I thought that not following the herd was "cool" so I wouldn't buy the latest rock album or see the newest blockbuster movie *on principle.* I missed out on a lot of good experiences with that ego-bound attitude! It was one rainy afternoon when a friend was delayed for a coffee rendezvous that I found myself outside a cinema showing "Jaws." Getting wet and with time on my hands I joined the queue feeling remarkably self conscious – and had a terrific afternoon! From then on, I gave things with "mass appeal" more house-room, although to this day I find myself thinking twice before purchasing something purely on the basis that "everyone" says it's good!

The key phrase in that last paragraph was "ego-bound." You can see how daft it would be if everyone adopted Wordsworth's philosophy and tried to go against the tide of opinion because going against the tide of opinion would quickly *become* the tide of opinion! (I imagine in this age of almost instantaneous mass communication it would be relatively easy to start such a movement! If you feel inclined to make a bit of social mischief, I've just given you a great idea. Just don't say it came from me – I'll deny everything!)

It isn't about proving something. It's about listening to your own instincts and inner wisdom – and trusting that. The key is in learning to become aware not of your thoughts – you won't have enough lifetimes to *reason* your way through every decision – but of your true feelings. If it feels good, go for it. Notice I said your *true* feelings. That means getting to know your true self a little better than you perhaps do now.

The more you listen to, trust and follow your own heart the happier you will be. And the easier you will find it to make decisions about anything.

We'll explore this in more depth later, but for now let's move on...

## *Getting To Results.*

What you and I and all the rest of us want is to get results. We want, as I have just said, to feel better!

When do we want it?

Now!

There is a huge myth – and a lot of unnecessary mystery – surrounding psychotherapy and any school of thought which claims to bring about rapid change in a person's psychological make-up. The myth was started inadvertently by none other than the great Sigmund Freud to whom we should all be immensely and eternally grateful, for without him we probably wouldn't have psychotherapy at all.

As well as being the grand-daddy of psychotherapy, his pioneering ideas were founded on a desire to "reverse engineer" the mind of the "patient" by digging deep into the subconscious and uprooting buried memories, along with fears long forgotten, the complex interpretation of dreams and so forth.

The patient might spend a decade or more in such "psychoanalysis" and there are plenty of practitioners, purists and patients to this day who swear that this remains the best route to go.

My question would be, "the best route to go *where*, precisely?" The required result is surely lasting change that feels better, and if we had to spend ten years at our doctor's surgery for every sprain and twinge we would soon get fed up with life I should imagine.

Assuming that you are with me on this line of thinking so far, then all you need is a basic understanding of yourself as a living person and member of the human race – nothing too philosophical I assure you – and you will have sufficient building blocks to construct and perform a "cure" for most troubles.

In fact, I can give you that basic understanding right now. It's this:

*You will, in common with all living things, go to extraordinary lengths to avoid pain, and to some considerable trouble to gain or sustain pleasure.*

There! That's it! All your behaviour, along with mine and all the other Homo sapiens you've ever encountered, is motivated by those two polar opposites. It's carrot and stick, if you will.

Now, of course, there is a little more to it than that, but only inasmuch as it helps to know exactly what you regard as pleasure and what causes you pain, (for which you may also read "fear", "anxiety", "self doubt", "embarrassment" and so on).

As I said, the only change you ever really want is to feel better. That is available to you right now, no matter what your circumstances. Mastery of the mind is perhaps the most neglected topic in any of the world's education systems. It hasn't always been so. In Georgian England, for instance, when small children were required to go to school for the very first time, their subjects included "kindness" and "manners." There was no sense of teaching them to read and write until much later in life.

I'm inclined to think that we have perhaps thrown the proverbial baby out with the bath water since Georgian times. Whilst today's teaching would be along very different lines, the basic notion that we are masters of, and not slaves to our moods and emotions has been seriously eroded if not lost.

Nowadays too, we are all too ready to blame DNA for our shortcomings, which is a more polite way, I suppose, of saying that it's all your parents' fault that you are as you are!

I fervently and passionately believe that there is virtually no characteristic, trait, habit or aspect of personality that any one of us cannot change if we so wish. This even includes our attitudes to "givens" such as aging. As I write this I am in my mid fifties, which means I have many friends of similar age. It is curious and somewhat bemusing to watch how we each handle the looming of old age. Some believe that decrepitude is inevitable and it is only the degree that will vary. Others, of whom I am one, believe that the number of birthdays you have had has very little to do with youthful spirit.

I can cite plenty of examples of people in the public eye who are fully functioning into their eighties and beyond. (I won't name too many here because as time passes more and more readers will raise their eyebrows with a quizzical "Who?") But I imagine the names of Bob Hope, Woody Allen and even Victor Borge may mean something for a generation or two yet.

That, I know, hardly constitutes scientific research. The good news is that plenty of science has been applied to the psychology of aging and it strongly suggests that a great deal of what we have taken as "inevitable" is far more due to following the herd thinking than to the actual deterioration of the body or brain.

So, self help may not only relieve you of worries, anxieties, fears, phobias, addictions and a string of other common woes, but may also keep you young to boot! What a bonus!

# A Word About "Alternative" Therapies

Before moving on to the meat of the book I thought it would be useful to put all of what you're about to read into some kind of context. As I write this in the Winter of 2010-11, there are countless "alternative" medicines and therapies on the market covering every kind of human condition you can think of – and a good many that you can't!

The word "alternative" however, disturbs me for two reasons. It means, in this context, that what the doctor will diagnose and prescribe for you is "mainstream" and that if you choose anything else then that is regarded as "alternative." The word has also acquired the connotation of being slightly "wacky".

The other, more pertinent reason that the word causes me to grimace somewhat is that it implies that, where medicine is concerned, which for us means pretty much exclusively psychological medicine such as anti-depressants and anxiolytics (anxiety relief such as Diazepam for example), that your choice is simply either/or. You take the doctor's advice and the little pills he prescribes, or you go to a merchant of something else which may be anything from a lot of talking to remedies made from ancient herbal recipes to old magic.

To my mind it is not like that at all. I don't like taking pills or medicines as a general rule, since I reason that my body cannot naturally "want" these powerful chemicals in it! But if I have a headache I have been known to resort to painkillers. If the headache wouldn't go away I'd go to my doctor first. That's *first*. I'd consider other options too.

The offerings in this book are not intended to be "either/or" in regard to your psychological well-being. The travesty and the tragedy I've witnessed countless times during my three and a half decades as a mental health professional isn't so much that people don't help themselves through mental tough times. It's much more that they believe they *can't*. You're depressed? Take Prozac, (or whatever the current drug of choice happens to be), or stay depressed! That is no choice at all.

When I was a mere stripling student psychiatric nurse I once asked a psychiatrist how a pill could possibly lift depression. I simply couldn't fathom how swallowing a chemical compound, which is physical after all, could possibly raise a person's spirits or mood, which is self evidently abstract.

He replied by telling me how the brain chemistry is different in a depressed person from "normal" and that the pills helped to restore that natural balance.

That sounds perfectly reasonable on the face of it. But only a few moments of reflection will reveal the flaws in his logic. For one thing, no one knows what "normal" is about most things to do with human beings. It's not "normal" to completely recover from "terminal" cancer, but many people do! Brain chemistry is still a relatively new science, so I doubt we're even close to really knowing "norms" of it.

The argument really falls down though once you start wondering about which is the chicken and which the egg in this scenario. Does a depressed person's brain chemistry change thus *causing* them to be depressed, or is it that the individual gets into some kind of downward spiral of negative thinking which then causes a measurable shift in brain chemistry?

In terms of the efficacy of the tablets, it makes little difference. It doesn't really matter where you break into a vicious cycle as long as you do break it. Take my earlier example of a painkiller for a headache as an example to illustrate my point.

If you have a "tension" or "stress" headache, effectively what is happening is this: You felt stressed, tense or maybe tired. As a result, you subconsciously tense up some muscles around your neck, eyes etc. which then go on to cause some pain – the headache.

In turn, the headache causes you to tense your muscles even more in a perverse attempt to control the pain. (Don't ask me why we do this. It's not a very helpful reaction to pain, obviously!)

Now we have a vicious cycle. The painkiller does not, as such, alleviate the headache. In effect, it mildly anaesthetises the nerves supplying those tense muscles enough so that you begin to relax them. As you do that, naturally your headache will subside because there isn't the tension to sustain it any more. By the time the painkillers' effects have worn off, your headache will have gone because you relaxed your muscles because they weren't painful any more … Get it?

Okay, it's simplistic, but as an explanation it should do the job.

An antidepressant medication isn't going to take all of your woes away. If you just lost the love of your life then that situation is still going to be there when the effects wear off! But you may feel better able to cope with it.

And *that* is the point.

The travesty and tragedy I referred to earlier is that millions of people currently believe that medication is the *only* thing that gets them through life. Such a belief utterly disempowers you as a human being, and by the way, massively empowers doctors and other health professionals who, no matter how caring or knowledgeable they may be, don't know *you* as well as you do. Only you can be the true expert on yourself!

Medication has a place. But you can do far, far more to help yourself through any situation, crisis, emergency, grief, worry, change, fear, anxiety … how many more conditions would you like me to name? … than you have ever dreamed possible!

Why is that important?

Because once you know you can pull yourself through life's turmoil and troubles, you feel:

- Empowered
- Proud
- Resourceful
- Energised
- Willing to try new things
- You dare to dream again
- You become an inspiration to others
- You start to get to know yourself better and take yourself to new heights
- … and you're no longer reliant on the doctor being available on demand or writing you repeat prescriptions for what is effectively more poison! And besides, one day he or she may tell you that you no longer need it!

You've invested in this book. You're open to new possibilities and change and new ideas just because of that. Good on ya!

If this is all new to you, take a few baby steps at first. If you'd bought a recipe book on how to cook cordon bleu recipes you wouldn't begin with the most complicated one unless you were already a competent chef, let's say. And if you've never cooked in your life, just try boiling an egg or heating up some spaghetti first!

See what I mean? I don't know where you are on your journey. I only know that through these written words we've met now and that means something to us both. Find your inner power and I promise you that through doing so you will also find your inner peace and your dormant dreams will begin springing to life.

There is no gift I can think of more valuable than that.

But if you are really struggling, please don't sit here staring at my words while you suffer in torment of some kind. Not if a trip to your doctor will sort it in a few hours or a couple of days. There's no guilt or shame in that!

You're on a journey of discovery – self discovery – possibly the most exciting journey of your life. Just be as gentle with yourself as you need to be, that's all I ask. Especially if this is your first foray into the exciting terrain of self help!

So plunge in and take from this book whatever you can. Plunder it, refer to it often, and pass it on to whosoever may need it. (Best to have a couple of copies because you're unlikely to get this one back!)

# 6: Effortless Creating Without The Law Of Attraction

I'm going to have to come clean. I confess I've told you a tiny lie. I don't feel too guilty about it though because I'd been telling the same tiny lie to myself for years before I realised what was going on!

Also, it's a very useful lie.

You see, I'd stumbled upon a powerful and pragmatic way to make things that I wanted come to pass in my life, yet when I came across the notion of "the law of attraction" I didn't believe it.

It was only later that I realised I didn't *need* to believe in the metaphysics that may or may not be what makes it work. Nor did I need to understand the very complicated quantum science that now increasingly backs up the ancient beliefs. Not only that, but now there are times when the science is actually leading the way.

These days, I personally do understand, believe and accept that the law of attraction is real and provable scientifically and subjectively. But it wasn't necessary in order to get results and it doesn't matter whether you believe in it or not.

This book will help you wherever you may be on that belief spectrum, but my intention in the main is to show you the way to effortlessly create your reality the way you want it without any need for belief in or understanding of the law of attraction.

I privately called what I'd "created" Supertherapy and it was doing exactly the same job as the law of attraction. In other words, I was getting results.

Let me give you one example. As you read, just count the "coincidences" in this true story.

After my first marriage ended I was left with a big empty house and a mortgage I could not pay no matter how I turned the numbers around. I knew, (logically), that the day would come when the house would be taken away from me – repossessed. It was as inevitable as sunrise – it was simply a logical mathematical calculation.

Logic, you will soon discover, plays little if any part in how things work out and so, although the concepts you are about to learn were very new to me, I kept a mental candle burning for finding a way to stay in my home.

Things were looking dire a month or so after I'd been left alone and one November evening there was a knock at the door. It turned out to be an ex-neighbour from the street I'd lived in before, wanting to drown some sorrows and have a "man's night on the town."

I was game for a beer and so we went out. Please understand that this man had never called at my new address before – and as it turned out, he never did again. But this one occasion was to change my life.

It was midweek and the streets of our little Bedfordshire town were almost empty, as was the pub we went to, save for a few "regulars." My friend could drink three pints to my one – a fact I already knew from previous experiences – and I was happy to let him drown his sorrows in this way. There was a pretty barmaid he'd noticed and he pointed her out to me. I judged him too drunk to make much impression on her and I hoped he wouldn't embarrass himself by trying to.

He didn't need to as it happened because in the next moment a man I'd never seen before walked in and spotted my friend. The two men greeted each other warmly. It turned out that they were old school friends who hadn't seen each other for years.

(Are you adding up the "coincidences"?)

This man had come to the pub, it transpired, to see his girlfriend who happened to be … the attractive barmaid!

As the pub was quiet, her boss allowed her to come out from behind the bar and have a drink with us. Of course, she was talking mostly to her boyfriend. My drunken friend tried to impress her by asking her what an intelligent, attractive young woman was doing "working in a place like this?"

She told him that she was a psychology graduate and had just been accepted to work in a place which she then told him the name of. That name meant nothing to him, but I knew what it was because it was a private psychiatric institution and I'd heard of it because of my work in the psychiatric health service at that time.

(Did you count the coincidence there?)

All three were astonished when I told them what it was – especially as it was the first time I had spoken since the young lady had joined us.

Now the young woman spoke to me ... and to cut a long story short, I ended up becoming her employer and ... her *landlord*. She was looking for a nicer place to rent than her current accommodation and of course I had a spare room! Her rent enabled me to pay the mortgage and saved my home.

---

Unless you're very, very different to anyone I've ever met, (and why would you be reading this book if that were so), you have hopes and dreams that you put on hold – maybe a considerable time ago, and you also have a bunch of negative beliefs that limit you and hold you back.

Topping that off, like the icing on an already undesirable cake you've been forced to eat, will be some very powerful reasons – which I call excuses and you'll forgive me later for that – such as your responsibilities towards your family, boss and bank manager, to name a favourite few. These you will hold aloft for yourself and anyone who challenges you as to why you are not living your dream life to see, and you will convincingly argue that he, she, they or it are the reason why your life is not all you would have wished it to be.

Yet.

So you keep dreaming, wishing and hoping.

But the dreams, wishes and hopes fade with each passing year.

So that's more or less where I imagine you to be in your life. You're by no means a failure, but you're not who, what or where you'd truly love to be. Does that about sum it up?

The question, then, is firstly, *could* change yet occur? Could you really have, be and do all of those things? Wouldn't doing so cost you dearly if you tried? Might you be risking your marriage, your life savings, not to mention your reputation to step out of the familiar and into the exciting unknown adventure called "your life"?

I'm here to tell you that I firmly believe you can have it all, and whilst some things may change, you actually will increase your "lovability" not to mention your personal self worth as you do so.

The second question is *how* to bring it all about? Who can help you overcome these obstacles which have so far stood in your way as surely as the Himalayas loomed before Hannibal?

The answer to that and all the above questions, plus any more that may have cropped up in your mind so far is, for many, both surprising and obvious.

The best therapist in the world is the person who knows you better than anyone. And that person is *you*.

Using my "SuperTherapy" principles, I will show you how to access your own inner strengths, resources, creativity, daring, *joie de vivre,* and blossom into your personal magnificence in a way no other self help book, recording or teacher ever has.

I know that's quite a claim, but I believe it's true because if you follow the processes I'll walk you through, (and they're a doddle), you'll experience the changes for yourself. It's second best only to being a participant in a live workshop.

It will motivate you, provoke you into positive action, inspire you, poke you, delight you and above all change you the way *you* want to be changed.

It will give you back yourself in such a way that you will become the clay with which you can re-sculpt and structure your own life. On your terms in your way at your speed. (But don't hang around; time is the most precious commodity you have. You'll never get today again).

The power of the self is immense, beyond the wildest dreams of your wild dreaming self even. This is not an ego trip, however. To access this power you will need to leave that aside. (I'll show you how). You will connect with a more spiritual side of yourself. You will listen to your emotions and learn to trust your inner guidance.

Perhaps for the first time you are truly going to wake up and smell the roses.

# 7: Your Power As A Human *BEING*

## Getting Results by the "Struggle & Effort" Method.

We who have grown up in Westernised cultures have a belief that is deeply ingrained that in order to *get stuff* we have to *do lots*. The whole of life is set up this way.

Think about it: from toddler-hood onwards you were told to study hard, work hard at school and eventually to get good grades, (or exam results as we call them in Britain).

Why do we want results like these?

So that we can get a "good" job, (that is one that attracts a salary that will allow us to acquire more "stuff" like a smart car and nice house usually with a hefty mortgage), and hopefully "settle down" and *have* a family. We will, of course, have to continue to work hard in the good job, and probably keep studying interminably if we have any ambition at all to climb whatever career ladder we've started on, or indeed, wish to switch to later in life.

Why do we want all of that? (Phew! I'm exhausted just writing about it – how did I ever do it?)

Well, we want all of that so that we can *be* happy. Oh, my giddy aunt! We could have been that all along!

My favourite story as a child was "The Wizard Of Oz." Poor Dorothy gets completely blown off course by a tornado, and gets side-tracked down the yellow brick road until she meets a charlatan wizard who looks like he can help her, (and does try, bless him), until eventually the woman (angel) who seemed at first to be little more than a second hand shoe giver, reveals that Dorothy has had the means to get herself home all the time.

The incantation, (magical chant), as you will surely remember, that Dorothy has to utter is, "There's no place like home." Home, of course, is where the heart is, and you can, like everything else, choose to put your heart anywhere that feels good to you. It isn't a building in Kansas or anywhere else – it's *inside* you!

The Wizard of Oz is a wonderful story because Dorothy's journey, (in which, of course, she and her companions discover a great deal about themselves, including that the only way they can even *believe* they lack the quality they think they most need is by having it in spades already), is the journey we all want to make: the journey home.

And yes, every one of us has a pair of those magical shoes! Except they're not worn on your feet; it's nothing more than the ability to change your mind. Now, I need to rephrase that or you'll almost certainly just skim over it and read on as if nothing just happened.

**The ability to change your mind is the most powerful life-engineering tool you possess.**

I'm not talking about you deciding to wear the blue shirt instead of the red one. That's the kind of "change of mind" most of us think of when we hear the phrase.

Can you imagine what it might be like to be a "shape-shifter"? You know, someone who can take on the form of an animal or even at object by changing the molecular structure of their body. So far, this is the stuff of science fiction and Super-Hero cartoon characters. But imagine the *power* of being able to do that!

That is the kind of personal power I'm talking about with your ability to change your mind.

Have you ever had an embarrassing experience and then said, "You know, one day I'll look back on this and laugh"? In order to do that, you had to change your perspective – your *mental* perspective – on the event and that changed your feelings about it.

Has anyone ever said to you, "I could never do your job"? Or maybe you've said that to someone. Over thirty plus years in psychiatric nursing, I've had that said to me many times. In the early days I thought people probably could. After all, they only needed training. But then I realised they couldn't because not only would they never put themselves through the training, *but they couldn't see themselves doing it in the first place.* In fact, they probably made some kind of "horror movie" in their head about what they imagined doing my job might be like. Besides, their *heart* wouldn't have been in it so it wouldn't have felt like home to them.

I'd be willing to bet, if you're over about twenty-one – and possibly much younger - there are plenty of things that you now do or like which once you said you hated. Think about music you thought you'd never listen to, hobbies you thought you had no interest in, fashions you never thought you'd wear … the list could include just about any aspect of life.

Somewhere along the line, you changed your mind.

There will be more potent examples too. How about childhood fears you've grown out of? Habits you've changed, such as addictions or nail biting? (I'm not passing any judgements one way or the other here – I just want you to start noticing how much you can change even if, at the moment, some of those changes wouldn't be your preference).

All you need to do is to make that process conscious so that you can do it at will. I should perhaps clarify that I'm not suggesting that the alternative to the "struggle and effort method" is to laze around on your sofa and expect the world to drop at your feet! I'm simply saying that the actions you take from now on – once you've learned the effortless way of getting results - will feel natural, spontaneous, exciting and struggle free.

If you want your past to stop driving you into a future that feels out of your control and unfulfilling, (if not downright miserable as it is in some cases), then you need to know how to change your mind at will and in ways that you want. This isn't some frivolous exercise about whether to have pork or beef for dinner; this is life changing. This will re-shape your destiny and put it under *your* control – perhaps for the first time ever.

And it's never too late! The great Richard Bach, author of "Jonathan Livingston Seagull" and other powerful, brilliant books, once observed that a test to discover whether the adventure of your life was over or not was to check if you're breathing. If you are, he said, it isn't!

By the time you are around your late twenties or maybe your early thirties, you should have the following:

A respectable job. ("Respectable" is usually a judgment made by your parents, which means they can speak of you proudly when they address *their* parents or any other judgmental member of the "tribe" you grew up in, such as neighbours, aunts and so on).

A nice spouse or partner. Although the status of your relationship and even the gender of the person you choose to spend your life with is now more flexible than at any time in history, there are still certain expectations of who it is really okay to be with – whether spoken or unspoken.

A home. You should have a mortgage and you ought to have been able to afford a decent deposit on it, due to your respectable job. Quite a bit of debt, as long as you are managing it, can almost qualify as something of a status symbol!

Money in the bank and no unmanageable debt.

Various trimmings, such as a nice car, moderately expensive holidays, (known as "vacations" or "leave.")

A good reputation. You must be of good character and never harm anyone or anything, even their feelings.

Respect of those who know you, especially your family of origin followed by your friends and colleagues.

Love of your spouse and, in time, your children, (if they're not born yet.)

So now we have the "formula." You have to *DO* a lot of stuff so that you can *HAVE* a lot of stuff, some of which is tangible, like your bank balance and your home, and some of which is intangible, like love and respect.

And what is the purpose of all of this? Well, it's sold to us as *"success"* but here again no one defines it. For some the measures of success are a certain level of income which in turn pays for a lifestyle that can include yachts, fast cars, luxury homes and other things that only a lot of money can buy. Love, and/or maybe a lot of sex may show up as a by-product of this kind of life, but it's certainly not a priority or guaranteed.

For others success is the achievement of virtually any self imposed goal.

I would like to propose a different definition, which is also adopted by many. How does this sound: -

*Success is being happy every day, which comes about as a result of following your dreams and enjoying both the journey and the realisation of them.*

In other words, true success is synonymous with happiness! However, our current formula is highly unlikely to take us there. Look at it! Whittled down to its bare essentials, it looks like this:

**DO stuff ➜ HAVE stuff ➜ BE happy.**

The goal of all of that hard work, then, is personal happiness.

Consider the following story-come-joke which you may have heard some variant of. It goes like this:

*A millionaire went on holiday to a Caribbean island. Every morning he would go jogging on the beach before breakfast. The beach was deserted at that time of day apart from one lone fisherman who sat with his rod cast out into the ocean.*

*After a few days, the millionaire decided to speak to the fisherman.*

*"I've seen you here every day," he said, "and I wondered why you are here each morning fishing so early?"*

*"Well, I love the solitude and the sound and smell of the ocean," the young man said. "And I can sit here alone with my thoughts and at the same time catch enough fish to feed my family for the day."*

*The millionaire was struck by the young man's intelligence and good manners and after a moment's thought he said, "You know I'm a very rich man. I could set you up in business. Would you be interested?"*

*The young fisherman looked slightly puzzled. "What would be the purpose of that?" he enquired.*

*"Then you could make a lot of money," the millionaire explained, a little taken aback at the question.*

*"And why would I want that?" asked the younger man.*

*"Well then, after you've worked hard for twenty or thirty years and made your fortune you could retire and do whatever you like."*

*"Such as...?" asked the fisherman.*

*"Well, you could spend your days quietly fishing on the beach ..."*

Happiness is a state of mind, not something indicated by our bank balance! But it is not only the goal – it's our natural state and our birthright. All babies are born happy. Animals are born happy. *Struggle, worry and effort are learned.* You will sometimes hear people using the phrase "living like animals" to describe a disgusting lifestyle but actually, left to their own devices, animals are very happy and content with their lives.

Sure, we expect – and can have – more from our lives, but that's because we can create and choose in a way animals can't. But struggling is not supposed to be the way to get there!

And so we need an alternative – a shift in our thinking. One which is simple to implement and understand yet which makes a profound difference in every area of our lives. A paradigm shift, if you will. We need a shift as monumental as when Newton realised that the force that caused an apple to fall from a tree was the same force that holds the Moon in place around the Earth. Once he had seen that, neither his life nor the whole of science could or would ever be the same again.

I am about to show you such a shift, but be warned. You may at first dismiss it as obvious or say that it is playing with words but isn't something that is going to make the kind of difference I am talking about.

If that is your reaction, or anything remotely resembling that, you will be wrong. Very, very wrong. See the shift in thinking, *then*, I beg you, spend some time absorbing and exploring the implications. Your life, I promise you, will never be the same again.

## *Effortlessness.*

Effortlessness doesn't mean doing nothing. Rather it's the Zen concept of "doing without doing." This is not a recipe for laziness! It is instead a formula for getting far more done than you may have ever dreamed possible. You will still engage in activity. It just won't feel stressful any more.

With that preamble done, here, without further ado is the shift in thinking. Upon this single but enormous block of truth you are going to rebuild every aspect of your life the way you want it to be. You will become master of your destiny.

The shift is to know that everything starts with *being*. (An anagram of "begin" as it happens, and the totally inadvertent "typo" I made as I wrote it!)

# Begin with Being!

Out of *who* you are, and *the way* you are will arise action – actions that feel good and which flow and that have positive effects upon others as you do them. (In much the same spirit as I am writing this book. I have a general sense of where I am going and the effect I want it to have on you, but I do not know until I am actually in the process of writing it quite how it will come out or how the sequence will show up. All of that, plus the initial seeds of ideas I had for the book, I just trust and follow).

From *being* then comes *doing*. Taking action and living from your heart in this way in and of itself will give rise to the manifestation of the path, the tools and yes, the luxuries you desire as you travel your path, will all show up.

In other words, the shift you need to make for a successful, fulfilling, prosperous and happy life lived on your terms is merely a case of shuffling the words so that the sequence is:

# BE ➔ DO ➔ HAVE

That's it!

That's *it??*

Yes. That's it – and it's *huge*. In order to *be* you first must know who you are. You must know where you belong in the universe. Then you must like who you are – not in an arrogant, egotistical way, but in a gentle, loving and spiritual way.

To *do* from this perspective means trusting your guidance and being willing to follow intuition, impulses and not necessarily the herd!

And *having* is not clinging or possessive. Nothing in the physical world is for keeps anyway, is it? It is a treading lightly feeling, a good feeling of gratitude for what is. I can assure you that as you live this way more and more shows up anyway.

This, as I've already pointed out, is not how we have been taught to live. But it is struggle free, joyous and rewarding in every sense of the word. Every day is a joy to live and every encounter uplifting for anyone whose life you touch as well as for yourself.

Prosperity and abundance flow easily to you and you have no fear of letting money or things go for you know they will always return multiplied whenever you need them – and often in such abundance that it is hard to know how to give it away.

Life is joyful and flowing and easy. Yes, you still have bills to pay, responsibilities to heed to, but there is no struggle, no sense of resentment. You won't be marking time until you can claim your pension. Your relationships blossom. Your creativity flows. You seem to have enough time for everything. Above all, your dreams become reality.

Does that sound like the kind of life you've always wanted? If so, then before going any further, ask yourself if you are prepared to read one single book, (this one), from cover to cover to achieve that glorious state.

Yes, I know it's easy to glibly tell yourself "yes" in your mind. No one's listening after all. But don't lie to yourself. (It would only be yourself). Because there's one more condition: you need to be willing to follow whatever instructions there are within the pages to come.

I promise you two things before you make that commitment:

1. You will not be required to do anything dangerous, immoral, illegal or fattening.

2. There is no condition, history or situation that you can bring to this life changing program, (for that is really what it is), that cannot be handled and healed by what follows.

Now you know. Beyond that you do not know, but then that's how life is anyway. None of us knows what's round the corner. Except death. (Which may turn out not to be so bad, but it's still a bit of a life changer.)

So, whilst we're here and alive, let's get on with living, really living, shall we?

Are you committed?

Then turn the page ...

# 8: The Foundation Stone: How to "Do" Being

Back in October of 2008, my main source of income was from agency nursing. I had worked for the same agency for eight or nine years and there had always been a steady flow of work. True, it was unpredictable – I never knew where I would be sent from day to day, and of course there was no guarantee that work would come in on any given day. But throughout any month there was always enough – and often more than enough – to pay the bills and have some cash left over for some leisure activities too.

But 2008 was also the year the banks of the world collapsed, if you recall. Whilst the health care industry was one of the lesser affected, (you can't stop funding hospitals), there was, nevertheless, a knock on effect. Agency nurses come at a premium for hospital managers, and they were under pressure to tighten their belts like every other drain on the economy.

The result, from my point of view, was that the phone simply stopped ringing. Not entirely, but nothing like before.

As the truth dawned on me and my wife that this could be a long term situation, we had the inevitable discussion any couple would have under similar circumstances: we sat down and asked ourselves, "What are we going to do?"

We weren't at the panicky stage, but we were concerned.

Over three days we toyed with various options. And then on the third day a light bulb went on in my head. As the same conversation began again I suddenly blurted, "Honey, you know, we're asking the wrong question!" I had remembered that I know a different way. (It is interesting to note how easily, under a little pressure, we revert to habitual thinking and patterns of behaviour, so take heed! You need to be mindful and aware, *especially* when you have a tough problem to solve, that you need to pause, take a step back and come at it from a different angle).

My wife blinked at me for a moment before asking, "So what question should we ask?"

I explained that we were repeatedly asking ourselves and each other what we were going to do, as if the repetition would somehow produce a result or an answer would reveal itself. Then I said, "We need to ask ourselves first how we are going to *be*."

You see, we were being worried, concerned and anxious. We kept looking at the problem. Neither of those approaches, alone or combined, would solve it.

"How shall we be, then?" my wife asked me.

"Let's be … resourceful and creative," I replied. "Even playful."

For the first time in three days we smiled at each other. "Okay then," she said. "What happens then?"

I made a few minor adjustments to my physiology, (I'll teach you how shortly), and *just a few seconds later* I said, "As my resourceful, creative and playful self I would ask, 'How many other ways could we come up with to bring in money?'"

Please understand that up until that point it had never occurred to either of us to ask in our heads or aloud anything other than, "How can I get more nursing shifts?"

This was a tiny shift in thinking, but it made all the difference as you'll see.

A brief and fun brainstorm ensued between the two of us as we came up with things that people would pay for at machine gun speed.

"Music, cooking, eBay, writing ..."

Now I can play the guitar, my wife cooks for a living, we've both sold things on eBay before and ... I've been a published writer several times and had been paid for it.

All were ways we could, potentially, bring in money.

(Actually, until we made the shift in our thinking I don't believe we had even considered that the problem was shortage of income. Until that point, we had seen it as "not enough work" which was a completely different – and limiting – perspective).

I virtually ran to my computer. I signed up with a website called elance.com (which I already knew of – it's a market where freelancers to put themselves up for hire) and I filled in my writers' profile.

If you know Elance you'll know that usually you have to bid on projects you want to be hired for and wait for the closing date and hope that you are picked.

But I didn't have to wait. When I awoke the next morning – that's the very next morning – and checked my emails I had been *invited* to take on a project for which the hirer paid me a thousand dollars!

---

Since this is a book about being, it seems somewhat paradoxical to start by giving you something to do. Techniques, per se, are only as useful as the passion and commitment you put into them.

However, this is a practical book as well as a theoretical one. It is my intention that by the time you have completed it you will not only understand what needs to shift in order to have your life the way you want it, but you will know how to bring that shift about.

This, then, is the most important practical chapter in the whole book. What it contains is a technique which is the basis of all and any change you may ever wish to make. It is a simple, powerful and immediate way to access your own inner power.

You need no hocus pocus, nor is there a requirement for you to believe or disbelieve in anything in order for this to work. You will, in fact, recognise the power straight away. For that reason you may be tempted to dismiss it as too obvious or simple, so I give you fair warning: read and apply this diligently, carefully and as often as necessary – and your life will change. That's a promise.

# 9: The Magic "Formula"

I have a cookbook somewhere in my kitchen that has a couple of recipes right at the start for basic stock and a basic white sauce. These are then used as the building blocks of dozens of gorgeous full menu recipes throughout the book.

That's what I'm going to give you here – not a sauce or a stock recipe of course – but a basic set of building blocks. Once you know these simple steps you will have power to transform virtually any situation at will. Believe me, this will put you way ahead of the crowd! Remember, most people are reacting to life, thinking they just have to cope with whatever shows up.

You are about to discover that to a much larger extent than you have probably ever dreamed, life is under your control.

(At this point, my workshop attendees sometimes ask, "Are you trying to say that I'm God?" There is a very important answer to that question which I will address later. For now, suffice it to say that I'm not suggesting that you can create a world or even a daisy, but you *can* choose whether you find yourself in a field of daisies or up to your ankles in cow muck!)

For reasons which may already be obvious to you, I'm trying to steer away from presenting you with a series of "how to" processes or techniques since they always have people wondering if they're "doing it wrong" or "not trying hard enough" when results aren't exactly as described or expected.

The "basic recipes" that follow do have to be demonstrated in a technique-type fashion, but when you stop to think about them for a moment, you'll realise that actually all they are doing is making you aware – that is *conscious* – of what you have been doing naturally, but *unconsciously*, all your life. This is very different from, say, learning to drive or to play a guitar, which are not skills you are born with; merely the potential is present.

So first you're going to learn how to manage your state, (which you can call your state of mind or your mood if you prefer). Once you can do this, you'll never again be able to say, "I'm just in a bad mood today," or "I can't help it; it's just the way I am.."

Be prepared, then, to ditch some old excuses. But along with that comes the incredible joy of choosing how you handle life. In fact, you get the joy of being joyful – and that also becomes infectious! You'll make a lot of friends, receive a great deal of thanks and praise as well as opening up a *universe* of opportunities that you just can't imagine from here!

Now, turn the page with care…

# *Boo!*

Scared you, eh?

Well, that's a bit tricky in a book, but maybe I've slightly amused you or confused you.

In any event, you were for a moment in a slightly different *state* to the one you were in before you turned to that page. Your body language or physiology would have shifted a little. Your inner dialogue would have changed to something like, "What the …?" and, although it would have been very fleeting and you would barely have noticed, for a moment your beliefs about me and this book may have altered just a tad.

You might have wondered if you were reading the right book, or if the author was a nutcase after all, or if there was some kind of trick or joke being played on you … I don't know of course, because I'm not you. But I am sure that your brain would have tried to make sense of that page.

Now, order is restored once more. You can see a page of text again and the tone of the words you are reading is more or less congruent with what you were reading before. No surprises here, so no change of state.

That kind of "state change" goes on all the time, every day, throughout our lives. We're used to it. Of course, you don't expect books to suddenly shout "Boo!" at you – unless it's Harry Potter you're reading perhaps – but every time you react to just about anything, your state will change.

Your lover hugs you tenderly before leaving for work. Your state changes.

Your kids yell at each other. Your state changes.

Someone jumps the lights as you're about to cross the road. Your state changes.

A friend confides some personal gossip. Your state changes ...

Sometimes you may even say, "I just woke up in a bad mood today ..." (This last example is going to teach us a lot ... keep reading!)

Now, although you'll recognise or be able to relate to most of my examples above, (and doubtless be able to think of countless more of your own), they all have one thing in common. They are all examples of you reacting to something. (With the exception of the last one).

What you perhaps have never considered, (most people haven't), is that the process works equally well in reverse. If you could learn to *manage* your state, think of the advantages:

> You'd be able to snap out of a bad mood at will.

> You'd be in control of your emotions in almost every situation.

> You'd be able to "induce" confidence in yourself whenever you needed to.

> There would be no limit to the range of emotions at your command. In fact, you'd be able to summon just about any feeling in a manner similar to a great singer being able to produce a note with her or his voice – on demand.

Now, some people are uncomfortable with this kind of practice, saying it's "manipulative." Well, have you noticed how your morning DJ, if you listen to a music or entertainment radio station of some kind, is cheerful *every single morning?*

His job depends on it! Of course, the men and women who gravitate to jobs like morning DJ probably do have a somewhat upbeat temperament to begin with. But year in, year out, it would be absurd to think they never have a "bad" day. Yet their job is to make people feel good – and to do so at what is, for many, a very stressful time of day too. There is *no way* they could manage that if they didn't know how to make themselves feel good!

Actors and entertainers of all kinds have to "manage their moods" in some way. Those who don't and who turn, as some sadly do, to drink and/or drugs, fail to be entertainers after a while. Instead they garner pity or anger from their once loving public who have to stand by, horrified, and watch their beloved heroes, heroines and icons destroy themselves. That is not state management!

Here, however, is the big point that the objectors miss. If you know how to run your own mind and moods, you are far less likely to have others run it for you! For example, you'll be able to make a more informed decision about whether to buy the latest hyped up widget that's being promoted all over the telly and the web in time for Christmas if you can distinguish the parts of the ads that are intended to be emotional triggers from the facts.

You'll be cooler, calmer, more collected. You'll end up knowing that there's nothing you can't handle. And no, it doesn't mean you'll live like "Terminator". It actually makes you more compassionate, more understanding and loving of life and the wonder of it all. But it also means that when and if you need to, you can walk away virtually unscathed from negative influences and people who would, wittingly or unwittingly, hurt you.

You become your own person.

You aren't "fazed" by authority figures or bullies any more.

Is this beginning to sound like a worthwhile skill set to master?

I hope so, because beyond it lies the real magic – even greater things than this are possible! Because once you know how to manage your state you also have most of the keys to living life on your terms.

In the end, the manipulators and the bullies and the negative ones simply stop showing up in your life. More and more good things start happening. At first, you can't believe your "luck" but soon enough, you'll start to accept it.

Then you go through a phase of "It can't last" but it does – and eventually you relax and simply enjoy life the way you always knew it should be. With one important distinction.

If you had had it all "handed to you on a plate" it wouldn't have felt nearly so good. This way, having come through struggle and out the other side, you will be ever thankful for it. In fact, the chances are, you'll want to show others how to have their dreams too. You'll become a philanthropist.

At the end of your days, you will not only leave this world a better person than you started, you will leave the world a better *place* than you found it – and others will be carrying on the inspiration you set in motion!

If you are looking for a meaning or purpose to your life, (and we all are), I think you would be hard pressed to find a better one than this.

I hope you agree.

## *State Changing For Powerful Results*

This is where the rubber meets the road. Practice what follows whenever and wherever you can. Imagine you are learning a musical instrument you love and badly want to master. To begin with your efforts will be a little clumsy and uncertain.

*That's okay.* That is no reason to give up.

As you get more used to it, of course it will seem easier and more natural. And there will be days when you forget or it just doesn't seem to come together.

That's no reason to give up or quit either.

In fact, there is *no* reason to quit doing this – ever.

The "instrument" you are on the way to mastering, and eventually becoming a virtuoso of is *life*. Your life! Why would you ever quit on that?

(The most common reason is that people don't believe it works. I will say more about that later, but for now please get this point firmly embedded in your mind: The worst that can happen is that you'll feel good a lot more of the time than you're accustomed to. Oh, what a shame!)

Here, then, are the three key elements you will use to change your state at will.

1. Your body.

2. Your internal dialogue/monologue.

3. Your beliefs.

You will need to bookmark this and the next few pages because these basic processes are the master key to all that follows.

## Your Body.

Your body both receives and expresses emotion. When you feel sad your body looks, feels and moves in a distinctly different way from when you are happy, joyful or ecstatic. Your body reacts to your mood, if you like.

The good news is, since you have a lot of control over your body, that the equation works the other way around too! In other words, when you change the way your body looks and moves, you feel different.

You only have to see a well drawn cartoon – a few pen lines on a page or screen, (think of Bart Simpson), to tell what mood someone is in. All emotions are visible through someone's body language and facial expression.

There are some subtler physical shifts too, such as breathing patterns, tone of voice and speed of movement for instance.

You should experiment with all of these and more details as they occur to you, but you have the main ones here.

Now, what most people don't realise is that emotional expression is a two way street. When you feel an emotion your body language changes. Everyone knows that! But did you realise that when you change the way you use your body, you change the way you feel too? (Try dancing for five or ten minutes if you don't believe me!)

So when you catch yourself feeling an unwanted emotion about anything, here is what you can do:

1. Catch yourself! You must become *aware* of your responses to things.

2. Ask yourself what emotional state you are in now. (That's the one you'd prefer not to have). Let's say, for example, it's confusion or frustration.

3. Ask yourself what emotion you'd rather have instead. Don't worry that your brain will try and tell you that you can't have that, just ask the question. Be insistent! "I'm feeling frustrated and I'd rather feel ... *satisfied.*" Let's say that.

4. Think of a time – any time – when you felt the emotion you'd prefer. In this example, think of a time when you felt satisfied with the outcome of something – maybe a plan you made or an idea that came to fruition – anything you like. It doesn't matter how long ago it was or how unlike your current situation it was – you simply want to access the *resource* of feeling that emotion.

5. Once you've captured a memory or several, imagine yourself back there and notice how you used your body. How did you move, breathe and hold your head and shoulders? What

expression did you have on your face? As accurately as you can, adopt the posture now. Don't expect the situation that's frustrating you to change – it won't, (not instantly in most cases, anyway). All you are doing is changing you. Equally, this doesn't mean that you now have to be satisfied with the situation you didn't like a moment before – that's not the object of this exercise either!

6. "Rinse and repeat." Just keep putting yourself in that new state as often as you can. What you will discover is that your *approach* to the situation will change. Often, this is reflected in the situation itself starting to change: someone begins listening to or adopting your ideas, or an obstacle – which may even have been in the form of a person or – heaven forbid – a *committee* – suddenly evaporate or do a U-turn ... something. In the worst case scenario, nothing will change but you'll still feel better!

In case you're finding this all a little difficult to believe let me tell you the reason for that. You're just *reading it!* There's only one way to test this out – and that is to get off your butt and move!

Dancing is an excellent and fun way you can test this out. As a method of perambulation, dancing is nuts! Anybody who chose to cross from one side of a room to another in such a bizarre manner should be in a circus! But of course we don't dance as a means of getting from one place to another, we dance because it feels *great.*

I'm not suggesting that you should dance as you read, but you can check out how you're sitting – or perhaps standing – as you read. Are your legs crossed? Are you frowning or smiling? Is your breathing deep or shallow? Is your posture generally open or closed? Try shifting just a little and notice how your emotional response can change instantly.

As you know, dance is used in tribal cultures too, both as celebration and as a state-altering process. Perhaps one of the best known, (although little understood), forms of dance as ritual are the Kurdish "whirling dervishes."

Try dancing any time but especially the next time you feel glum! Put on your favourite dance tune, (it can be anything as long as it has a good beat and you love it – even if it's an old Bay City Rollers tune), and just dance around your living room, kitchen, bedroom – even your garden if you like – for three minutes or so. It is *impossible* to feel the same way when you do that!

Now, I do realise that if you should suddenly find yourself overwhelmed with stress in the middle of a company board meeting, it's hardly good form to pull out your iPod and blast out "Blame It On The Boogie" for five minutes. Well, not in any of the companies I've ever worked with it wouldn't have been, anyway.

But you can take a deep breath. You can smile too. Really, try smiling! Smile warmly at someone – someone you like, preferably; a random smile at someone you hate may be seen as sarcastic! But smiling releases endorphins, ("feel-good" chemicals), in your brain, and if done nicely will make you and at least one other person feel good. If you're on your own, smile a really big, broad grin, no matter how silly it feels! And remember, you don't have to have a "reason" to smile. It's better than free drugs, so make use of it!

You can also square your shoulders, marginally increase your pace if you're walking or running, relax your forehead or give yourself a gentle hand massage – just as a few examples.

If at this stage you still have a thousand questions that's fine. You may well still be wondering "What if it never works?" and "How can something as simple as changing my body language cause the whole world to change around me...?"

Right now, I just want to show you that you *can* change yourself at will. There's a lot more to come ... and all of those questions and many others will be answered as you go through the book. Remember what I said about the recipe book with the basic sauces near the beginning? All those great recipes for the sumptuous and delicious menus you desire are on their way.

## Here is a simple formula for shifting your body in order to change the way you feel:

1. Catch yourself feeling the way you *don't* want to feel. (Remember I told you that there's a kind of "watcher" you that isn't your body, thoughts, feelings etc? It's what enables us to be *self* aware – something which, as far as we know, no other creature is)

2. Label that feeling. What do *you* call it? Is it stress, worry, anxiety, depression...what?

3. Decide what would be, (for you), the *opposite* of that feeling. Again, there are no right or wrong answers – your answers are the ones that count. So for you it might be "calm" whereas for someone else it could be "resourceful" or "creative."

4. Think of a time when you were in that desirable state – even if only for a moment. In the unlikely event that your brain tries to convince you that you have never experienced that particular

emotion, then think of someone – even a fictitious character from a movie or even a cartoon – whom you consider exemplifies and personifies your chosen state.

5. Adjust your body *into* that state. How did you – or your character – move? At what speed? How did you (or they) hold their neck, what was the expression on your (their) face? How did you/they breathe?

Get it as complete and accurate as you can. You'll be amazed at how swiftly you start to feel better. The shift into the new state is, in fact, almost instantaneous!

Of course, you can just as easily slip back into the old pattern. In fact, you almost certainly will for a while. That's okay – as soon as you catch yourself doing it, just go through this process again. Remember what I told you about exercising new muscles?

Patience, my friend. You will soon be a master chef of life!

## 2. Your Internal Dialogue/Monologue

We all talk to ourselves – yes, even you! Some of us do it out loud more than others perhaps, but there's that "self-talk" going on in your head all of the time, apart from during sleep and maybe meditation or other very quiet times if you are someone who has learned to indulge in a practice such as that.

In our modern culture, with its 24 hour buzz of everything from news to entertainment in and out of our homes, it's all too easy to keep our heads filled with never-ending fluff and nonsense and never really to hear, let alone to listen, to our own thoughts.

That, as you may have suspected, is all about to change! (For you, that is!)

Once again, you will need to "catch yourself" in the act – just start to listen to what you say to yourself when, for example, you are faced with a task or project you don't like. Can you hear, inside your head, something along these lines, perhaps...?

> *"I'm no good at this type of thing."*

> *"I hate jobs like these..."*

> *"Joe Bloggs is always really great at this, but I just can't do it..."*

> *"I was always hopeless at [FILL IN THE BLANK] at school..."*

> *"It just isn't me ..."*

And so on. You get the picture. Of course, the inner chatter won't stop there. If someone were to ask you what you didn't like about the job, you'd rattle off a whole stream of well rehearsed and highly believable excuses that would "justify" (at least to yourself), why you were not good at whatever it is.

This isn't to say that you should now take on everything that lands on your plate. Or desk. I like to avoid the word "should" wherever possible – those kind of self imposed rules can really ensnare you.

What I want you to realise is that you *could*. You have a choice. I know that I *could* service my car when it needs it, but I learned a long time ago that whilst it can save me money that isn't my priority. I'd rather pay a professional to do it while I stay at home and write my book, or whatever I'm doing at the time that feels good. I just don't love fixing mechanical things.

Right, so the next thing is to get *playful* with your inner dialogue! Think of it this way: a voice is living rent free in your head! No, that doesn't mean you have a mental health problem – we all have this going on. Trust me; I'm a mental health professional!

Notice what tone the voice has. Do you generally scold yourself? *("How could I have been so stupid??")* Hardly anyone has a habit of patting themselves on the back or giving out self-praise. It's definitely a pattern you should practice!

How about the volume? What direction does it mostly come from? Is it located inside your head, or somewhere outside? (Don't panic! Everyone's different, and there are no right or wrong answers here. Besides, you don't have to send in a report – you're the only one who's ever going to know!)

Once you've established a few characteristics of the voice, start to play with it. Imagine you have a very sophisticated remote control wand. Let's change the tone of that voice to a smooth, sexy one! Or a cartoon one – how about Bugs Bunny's nasal tones?

Turn the volume down low. Imagine late night jazz playing in the background, (or if you happen to hate jazz, you can use Mozart or Take That or anything that makes you feel good when you hear it).

Play with the direction control too. Can you imagine the voice coming from the tip of your nose? Pretend you're a really top class ventriloquist and you can throw your voice anywhere. What if it came from the Moon, or the corner of your wardrobe?

I know these kinds of games sound a little ridiculous – which is precisely the point. By the time you've finished messing about with them, you're going to feel totally different about the issue you started with. I've had people collapse into fits of giggles trying to get the voice to come from their nose tip – and the issue they began with seemed pretty serious to them – only minutes before!

Of course, they – and you – will still be able to recall exactly what happened or what is happening. But now your reaction will be different. You will no longer be paralysed by an emotion such as fear and you will at the very least have choice about how you respond.

And yes, I have used this technique (combined with others) on some very "serious" issues, such as rape or abuse. Such events do not have to rule your life. (More on powerful change and trauma resolution later ...).

## 3. Your Beliefs

There have been times during my career as a workshop presenter when I've just wished I could shout from the top of my lungs, "For goodness' sake, stop believing everything you think!"

You will never meet anyone who agrees with you about absolutely everything, will you? Does that mean that you're the only one who's got everything right? Or, conversely, does it, as some people with self esteem issues believe, mean that you have an awful lot of things wrong and other people know best about loads of stuff?

No, no and NO!! It means nothing of the kind!

You have your own set of beliefs, but if your life isn't working out the way you'd like it to in some area(s) then check out what you believe about things.

For example, I used to believe that I had to have a "good career." My father told me so. Neither of us ever defined what "good" would mean in this context, but I took it as read that I had to have a "respectable" job, (which means other people would think well of me), and that it should be "secure" (meaning that I could earn money as he did until I was almost ready to drop), and so on.

I became a nurse, and I have to admit there's a lot about that profession that I enjoy. By no means everything, though, especially with its rigid medical model. When I was accepted for nurse training in 1976 my father was pleased. He said I had a job for life. Within a decade, Mrs. Thatcher was Prime Minister and nurses' jobs would never have the same security again. Irony of ironies!

Happiness, fulfilment and passion for what you do in life were values that came low on my father's list. I don't blame him; he was a product of his generation and he had survived the War too. Happiness was something you got in small and random doses if you were lucky, maybe on holiday, (two weeks a year at best), or when you retired if you lived that long. Life was otherwise just hard work.

I'm sure I don't need to give you chapter and verse about my early family life for you to get the message that there were a lot of "taken for granted" family beliefs that I later came to question. Maybe my own son will one day question mine, if he isn't already. That's okay – this is his life.

Deep in my soul, though, I always wondered why people just couldn't do what they loved. And when both my sister, aged five, and my mother, aged forty, died within two years of one another, I, aged nine, began to ask a lot of questions about how and why I was going to live *my* life.

What, then, is the message here? Well, first of all it is that no one knows better than you what you believe or what *to* believe. Someone else's views may highlight an issue for you, or make you think differently, but the only hero to have in your life in the end is yourself.

You have two kinds of beliefs – global and personal. Examples of global beliefs would be "war is bad" or "the rich get richer while the poor get poorer." (Both of which have powerful counter-arguments by the way, as all beliefs do. There is no such thing as *the* truth!)

A personal belief might be, "I'm just not lucky in love" or "I was never any good at maths."

Now, as you can see, beliefs such as those are not going to serve you well if you meet someone you're deeply attracted to or you get offered a dream job on the proviso that you can do the company accounts too!

I am going to suggest a handful of generic positive beliefs you might adopt, but if you think of some of your own that cover any ground you want, by all means use those instead, (or as well).

Here are a handful that have served me well in all manner of circumstances over the years. They are not all my originals, but I'm certain that the people from whom I learned them won't mind me passing them on. I rather think that was the idea anyway. Here we go:

- The past does not equal the future.
- There's always a way if I'm committed. *(Thanks to Tony Robbins for these.)*
- Whatever happens, I can handle it. *(Susan Jeffers – thank you too.)*
- There is no reason for me to feel bad – ever.
- There is *always* a choice.
- I am free – always.
- If I feel passionate about doing something, I can achieve it.

How do you adopt a new belief, I hear you ask? The simplest way is to do it the way you adopted the originals – by repeating it over and over in your mind. Ironically, you won't believe it at first; your ego mind will just dismiss it with inner dialogue roughly the equivalent of a sardonic, "Yeah, right!" Silently thank that voice and persist.

After a while, that begins to take root in your mind, and your brain will begin to look for evidence that your new "mantra" is true. (This is how all beliefs get established).

Tony Robbins gives a wonderful example in some of his talks about this. He asks you to consider if it is true that human beings are inherently bad or evil. It is relatively easy to construct an argument for this premise, and people begin responding with examples of the Holocaust, terrorism, child abuse – I'm sure you can think of plenty of examples.

He then asks if it is true that human beings are inherently kind and loving, and immediately people start talking about charity work, Mother Teresa, Ghandi and so on.

It quickly becomes apparent that neither premise is *globally* true. Sometimes, some people behave in certain ways, and other times they behave in other ways is about all you can say – which is pretty meaningless. But imagine how your decisions would differ and how you might behave differently if you fervently held to one extreme belief or the other.

Repetition works, but it can be slow. (It might take a few days – maybe even a couple of weeks – for a new belief to "bed in"). If you want to fast track your new belief, combine it with the state management process and adjust your body, (physiology), so that it matches – as nearly as you can manage – that of someone who believes what you'd like to believe. It doesn't matter if you don't know anyone personally with that belief – you can adopt the physiology of Superman if you like, as long as you don't try to fly!

I am immensely grateful to a vast number of teachers, from authors living and dead, (Alan W. Watts, Carl Jung, Wayne Dyer, Deepak Chopra and Gill Edwards to name but a handful), as well as personal friends who have taught me immensely important things.

I recall the liberating feeling when I read somewhere that we should all read the great religious texts *as critics*. The wisdom in them is priceless and wonderful – and also *millennia* old! The only "gospel truth" there really ever can or should be is your own. Or maybe that there is no fixed gospel truth!

Now all of that comes with a heavy responsibility. It means you have to think for yourself. What do you and don't you actually agree with? Wow, that's enormous!

Fortunately, there is a short cut.

You simply need to notice if something *feels* good and right to you. To me, it did not feel quite right that I *should* be tied to a job for forty years when there were so many other things I wanted to achieve in my lifetime. It took me a few of those years to acknowledge to myself that I didn't feel too good if I told myself that I *have* to have a job, but once I saw that there were alternatives – and that it would be perfectly okay for me to try some of them - I was liberated.

Once again, it's about becoming aware. Listen to, check in with, and acknowledge how things *feel* every step of the way. If something really feels good – like it makes you want to sing and you can't wait to get out of bed in the morning to do it – then do it. If, on the other hand, you're moaning and complaining and feeling envious of people who've got something or some kind of life that you'd rather have, then stop your whingeing and start changing. That can be yours too!

The only person stopping you is yourself, and you're doing that with your negative and unnecessary beliefs. But we're getting ahead of ourselves. All of that and a great deal more is going to be covered in the pages that follow.

# Installing A New Belief

There are a great many processes I've come across regarding how to change your beliefs, from simple mind tricks you can do as you're driving, jogging or just taking a shower, to subliminal messages embedded in New Age music or even recordings that claim they are synchronising your brain hemispheres.

I don't want to disparage any of these – I've tried several different methods myself over the years, with varying degrees of success, and pretty much all, I'd say, had at least the result of giving me a nice warm fuzzy feeling.

The problem, however, was twofold. First, getting the new belief *in* didn't seem nearly as difficult as getting the old one *out*. Each time I'd think I'd done it, a situation would crop up and there would be the old behaviour pattern, (and hence the underlying belief), once more.

The second problem was identifying the belief I apparently didn't want in the first place. Since my beliefs are lodged, I am repeatedly informed, in my subconscious, how on earth am I supposed to bring them to consciousness? And even when I do manage to catch a fleeting glimpse of a passing negative belief, how can I be sure I've uprooted the whole undesirable weed of a thing?

I'm a great believer in there being a simple way with such things. Elusive though it may have seemed, (and I do own that I have a tendency to "over-think" things sometimes), I just *knew* there had to be an easy and fast way to change beliefs.

It turns out, thank goodness, that there is.

I'd like to explain it with an analogy of recording onto tape, but since recording tape of all kinds is already fading into the annals of history as I write this in 2011, I can hardly expect that any reader will have a clue what I'm talking about should this book be so fortunate as to still be around in a generation's time!

Right now, I can talk of hard drives, although I'm equally sure that they too will be superseded by some other hitherto undreamt of technology, so I will just have to assume that there is some recognisable medium onto which data can be recorded – data such as sound, moving or still images and, of course, words – and which can also be *over-written*.

With cassette tapes or video tapes you simple re-used them and whatever had been there before was wiped clean and replaced with the new recording. Now we use hard drives which are a little more hidden from our view, (so you can't see a tape with an old label that has been scribbled out half a dozen times), but the principle remains the same. In some ways, hard drives make a better analogy because of course our computers run software installed on them.

The computer will run whatever program you decide and it will then run that program according to however the programmer has written it. Sometimes "bugs" are discovered within the program, or an update is required for some other reason, and the writers or distributors release a new version. Installing the new version then *overwrites* the old one – and the old one simply isn't there any more.

Aha! Analogy made! There is no requirement to go digging around to erase the old files – regardless of the medium involved. Once you've installed the new one the old will self-erase!

Goody!

So now all we need to do is to know how to install our new belief. There is no longer a need to worry about "uninstalling" the old one. How then, does the mind allow this to happen, since we don't have an instruction manual for it?

Or do we?

Well, we know enough – in fact, more than enough. We know that we are motivated by pleasure and we are also motivated to move away from, or avoid, pain. We also know, and it is well documented, that the brain cannot tell the difference between something vividly imagined and the actual event. Chemical and physiological reactions take place in just the same way as if your body was actually performing the actions.

(Yes, in theory, you can even go jogging in your mind and still get fit. I haven't tried it, but I have heard of trials with basketball teams where one group physically practised whilst a second only mentally rehearsed their moves. A third group did neither. I think this was done for a six week period. Both the "rehearsed" groups had improved by the same amount, whilst the third group of unrehearsed guys had lost their edge. Makes you think, eh?)

So, all you need to do is to imagine as vividly as you can that you are doing whatever it is you'd do if you had the new belief. It is, quite literally, "make believe!" If you find this idea a little absurd, or you think you might just give it a try tomorrow, then go to the other end of the spectrum like this:

Sit quietly where you won't be disturbed for a good ten minutes or so. Now imagine how things will be if you *don't* change. How will it affect you as a person, your integrity and values? How will it affect those you love and care about? How will your mental and physical health suffer?

How about if you don't change for a year, or five years or ten?

How about if you *never* change? What will people remember about you and say about you after you're gone?

When that starts to smart, you'll have a go at the alternative! (See? I told you we'd do almost anything to avoid pain!)

The key to power here is your *imagination*.

Just spend a moment or two reflecting on why nature might have equipped you with an imagination. I don't suppose sabre-toothed tigers or dinosaurs sat around conjuring up their next hunt or mating experience any more than my domestic cat does nowadays.

Animals may be great survivors and they are certainly far more intelligent than they are mostly credited with being, but when it comes to imagination they just don't cut the mustard! In a million generations, even the great apes haven't thought of fire, although it's true that some of them do use tools.

So maybe I owe them an apology along with a few anthropologists I've inadvertently upset. My intention here isn't to be scientifically accurate: it's to make a point. *You,* along with all the other humans, can imagine *anything.* You can imagine a pink zebra if you want to, and you can certainly imagine yourself in a decent relationship or living a luxury lifestyle or in excellent health. Those are possible for you.

Now, what usually happens at this point is that resistance kicks in. Don't worry, it does for me too, but the difference between us these days is that I recognise it and know how to deal with it immediately. So let me teach you how to do the same.

Once you know how to do that, then we'll return to put the icing on the cake and I'll show you precisely how to install a new belief. (You won't believe how simple it is!)

## *Anchoring.*

Remember the smell of freshly baked bread? What does it remind you of? What was your favourite hit record the first time you fell in love? What was the first movie you saw that made you cry?

In NLP triggers like these are called "anchors." If you already know NLP then this section will be a little refresher for you. And if you don't, this is going to be a revelation!

When I first heard about anchors I couldn't see what use they'd be. After all, I couldn't conjure up the smell of freshly baked bread at will, (unless I set about baking some bread of course), and so the memory would not be triggered. Eventually the penny dropped. You aren't waiting for the trigger – you are going to create your own triggers – or anchors – to fire up any emotional state you desire at will.

There is a neat and powerful trick you can do with anchors too called "collapsing anchors" – which I'll also show you. Collapsing anchors instantly and permanently *eradicates* unwanted responses. This is the way NLP earned its reputation for fixing phobias in minutes. (Yes, you will know how to do that very soon.)

Just to be sure that we are clear on the definition: an anchor is a trigger or a reminder of something that would, in the normal course of events, be otherwise unrelated to one another.

For example, the smell of freshly baked bread is just the smell of freshly baked bread. It doesn't remind everyone of their childhood. For some it may trigger happy memories, whilst other people may have less joyous recollections.

Advertising jingles are great anchors, and it will depend on your age and the culture you grew up in which ones trigger memories for you. Similarly, old TV theme tunes can have the same kind of effect.

Okay, now let's suppose you're invited for an interview for a job you'd dearly love to have. You know there are one or two serious rivals and you haven't done so well in recent job interviews. What you need is a shot of confidence!

No problem, Batman! Give yourself fifteen minutes of quiet time, (that means turning phones off these days), and do this.

Sit with your eyes closed and think of a time – even a moment – when you felt confident. It can be about anything. It could be crossing the road if you can't think of other examples, but there will almost certainly be more.

To help you, think of things you can do – such as riding a bicycle, swimming, knitting, cooking a meal, a time when you plucked up courage to ask someone on a date, a sporting event you won, an instrument you can play, a poem you recited by heart to an audience … that's enough … you're on your own with examples from here!

Now, once you've got something, (and if you really, really can't think of a single example then use the Superman trick I mentioned in the section on beliefs), and recall the moment/event as vividly as you can. Remember the sights, the sounds, the smells. The tones of people's voices. If it helps to increase the intensity of the experience, try zooming in on the "pictures" or brightening the colours. Put yourself back in the image as if you are seeing it all again with your own eyes rather than watching yourself as a spectator. You want to be *associated* with this experience.

Once it feels really good, keep your eyes closed and reach up with your left hand and pinch your left earlobe for about three seconds. That's 1 …… 2 …… 3 …. (If you're left handed you might want to reverse that instruction).

Now open your eyes. And then close them again. And now bring to mind *another* time when you felt the supreme confidence. Yes, you can find one. Usually, though not always, once you've found the first one, dozens more will start to pour through, a bit like when someone tells a joke and it reminds you of all the ones you couldn't remember for the life of you until they said it.

Pinch your earlobe again *in exactly the same way as you did before.*

And now do all of that a third time, making sure that you open your eyes briefly between each part of the process.

Okay, now you can test it. Close your eyes one last time and simply pinch your earlobe *in exactly the same way as before* and notice what changes occur in you. If you have done the exercise as I've described, you'll get a little surge of confidence.

Congratulations! You've created an anchor! When you pinch your earlobe, that's called "firing the anchor."

You don't have to use your earlobe. Some people like to pinch a knuckle, and admittedly you have more of them to choose from than you do earlobes, so you can attach a whole bunch of desirable states to your knuckles, but I like the earlobe thing because it only engages one hand, (you can do it even whilst driving), and with a little practice it looks natural so no one will notice if you do it mid-interview. Pinching your own knuckles looks a touch awkward to me.

I promised I'd tell you how to deal with phobias, and honestly people think this is real magic, but it is simplicity itself. Essentially, you are going to do the same as before, only now you need two anchors. Here are the steps.

1. First, with your eyes closed as before, you need to recall a time when you experienced the phobia. This will be a little uncomfortable of course, but it's only for a few moments and you know you can open your eyes at any time.

So recall it as vividly as you can, and when it's pretty intense reach up with your *right* hand and pinch your *right* earlobe for 3 seconds.

Then open your eyes.

2. Now ask yourself what feeling you'd like to have *instead* when you are in the presence of whatever it is that makes you phobic. It might be anything, but make sure it's couched in the positive: there's no such feeling as "not afraid." Let's suppose it's "calm."

3. Follow the procedure exactly as before – finding three memories when you experienced complete calm or serenity or felt at peace … they will all do the job! Each time, as before, open your eyes between anchorings, and of course, use your *left* hand and earlobe for each positive anchor.

4. Here comes the magic! Close your eyes one last time and pinch your *right* earlobe and whilst still holding that pinch, reach up and pinch your *left* earlobe so you are holding both at the same time. (There should be a moment between pinching the right and the left – about a second).

Because you have "stacked" three positive experiences on the left earlobe, your brain has more associations with the good feeling and is unable to hold both reactions at the same time, and the negative phobic reaction will be wiped clean!

Release the *right* earlobe slightly before the left, so that the "good" feeling is left lingering like an echo.

You can test the effectiveness of the process by closing your eyes one last time and imagining yourself in the presence of whatever used to trigger the phobic reaction. Although not everyone feels totally at ease, there is almost always a sense of being able easily to cope.

I once did this process with three women friends, all of whom told me they would run screaming from a room if they so much as *thought* a spider was present. When I saw them a few weeks later, in mid-September, the height of spider season, I asked them if they'd noticed any changes, and all of them said they hadn't seen any spiders since our encounter to test the theory! I find it hard to imagine that none of them had been near a spider, especially as we all live in the countryside!

Although there are plenty of alternative processes you could use, this simple anchoring principle works with any negative or undesired emotion or response. If you had a bad or traumatic experience that still haunts you, run through the same procedure.

First, name the main (undesirable) feeling that comes up. Then decide on how you'd like to feel instead. If nothing obvious springs to mind, or the traumatic memory is too overwhelming, choose "giggling" as your alternative. Just recalling all the silly times something or someone made you giggle is virtually irresistible.

Then, simply anchor the undesired emotion once – you will need to recall the event but only briefly. Think of it like an injection: it hurts when it goes in your arse, but boy you feel better afterwards!

Open your eyes and close them once more and bring to mind a time or event or person that made you giggle. Once you've got the giggles, anchor that on the other earlobe, knee, knuckle or whatever part of your anatomy you've chosen this time.

Do that last instruction twice more so you've "stacked" the anchors and then, finally "fire" both together.

You'll find the "traumatic" memory has lost all its power!

---

And *that's* all the NLP you need! If you want to study the subject in more depth there are a ton of books, DVDs and courses you can get involved in – but none of that is necessary for our purposes.

The simple truth that turns these techniques into a "magic formula" is that you have the ability to change your mind. I want you to *know* with the same degree of certainty that you have about how to clean your teeth that *you* and nothing and no one else are in charge of what you think, believe and feel.

Let me say it again. You have the ability, as a human being, to *choose what to think.*

This simple yet astonishing fact should, in my humble opinion, be taught in kindergartens throughout the world. If we had understood and utilised this power from the time we were children the world would be a very different place.

Depression, anxiety and stress would be virtually eliminated at a stroke. Relationships would stand a much better chance of survival. Even conflict, such as war itself, might be averted as world leaders would know how, and be expected by the electorate, to exercise their power to choose different ways of looking at situations. In fact, it's conceivable that the warring factions might size one another up differently to begin with.

Disney-esque fantasies?

I only ask that you don't judge yet. The potential is *at least* that great, so imagine what you are going to be able to achieve in your own life!

Okay, so you can choose what to think. *Big deal.* That used to be my reaction, and not surprisingly, it was the reaction of many of the groups I taught this to back in the late 1980s and early 90s. I used to just skim over the notion – mentioning it because somehow I sensed that someday it would become important.

It never occurred to me in those early days of my teaching that the idea would eventually take centre stage in my life. How many times have you said or heard someone say, "Oh, I've tried everything. I just can't …" You fill in the blank. It could be "lose weight," or "get more confident," or "earn more than this amount" or "find love" or "get rid of this disease/disorder/nervous tic …" and so on.

Millions of people are walking the Earth as I write this believing that some part of their life or other is fixed and stuck and that's that. Make the best of it.

I know we're still in the early pages of this book but I do want to shoot those ideas dead right now. They are, it turns out, total bullshit – if you'll excuse my language.

For a start, nobody's ever tried *everything*. It's so glib and easy to say and we, listening to our struggling friends, are inclined to shake our heads in sympathy and bewilderment. After all, if someone really has tried every solution possible to a problem then really there is nowhere else to go. What is there to say to someone who's just told you they've tried "everything"?

If you're honest with yourself, you might admit to a nagging doubt that your friend can't have tried absolutely everything because didn't Joe Bloggs have a very similar problem? He figured out a way to get rid of it! And then you shake your head. *"Nah! Can't have been quite the same in Joe's case."* And life moves on, unchanged.

My strong advice is that next time you hear someone say it, (and it could be you), just challenge that for a moment. Interrupt that line of thought with this simple question: "Are you sure that's true? I mean *everything* would be a heck of a lot of things to try!"

Of course, I don't mean to be too hard hearted about it. The person genuinely feels stuck with the problem. The statement, "I've tried everything" is really code for, "I'm afraid to try again because I've failed so many times and I can't bear the thought of doing that again. I'm scared of feeling guilty, angry with myself, disappointed and a failure in the eyes of people I love."

Those are most certainly powerful reasons to resist trying again. They are still, at root, however, bullshit because they're excuses. Not excuses of the nature, "the dog ate my homework, sir," because even the owner of the excuse believes it to be real.

I will show you in this book how easy it is to walk away free from any "problem".

Which brings me to the second point regarding why choosing your thoughts is so vital.

It's because the alternative, the much vaunted, praised and lauded alternative, is to make a lot of noise through activity – that is struggle and effort. In other words, we believe we have to *do* stuff. (Remember? We're conditioned to think we have to *do* so that we can *have* in order to *be* happy and successful!)

Fear not – I'm not advocating loafing on the sofa for the rest of your days, and neither will I be proposing eighteen hours a day of meditation and prayer. (Although fifteen to twenty minutes of daily meditation is something I both recommend and practice).

We do need to take action – but that will be action born of inspiration and passion and love for what you're doing, not the kind of activity we're so accustomed to which is done with a sigh, half a heart and all too often with a grudge. Action follows thought – and the thought must feel good first!

## How to Use These Processes...

When you come to the chapters that have to do with getting the life you want – such as wealth, health, happiness and so on – use the state changing process *first*. Think of the feeling you want – perhaps "vibrantly alive" or "full of beans" for the health chapter as examples. Use words that evoke a good feeling for you! Practice using the three elements of the state management process – shift your physiology, check your inner dialogue, and especially if it won't come or you experience any kind of resistance to making the shift – just ask yourself what you have to believe in order to keep the less desired state going?

Keep practising!

It may feel a little odd at first – in fact I'd be surprised if it didn't. But then, so did driving or swimming without floating aids for the first couple of times. Don't let that be your excuse for not doing anything!

When a state feels good – whether it's one you've deliberately placed yourself in or just one that happens along during your day – *anchor it*. You don't have to use your earlobe as I mentioned before; squeezing a knuckle is fine or pressing a finger to the tip of your nose – whatever works for you.

It's okay to choose one place on your body to anchor all the good feelings. So, for instance, you might decide the middle knuckle of your left index finger is what you're going to squeeze and you can do that when you feel ... inspired, courageous, grateful, delighted ... and so on. Just keep stacking them, and soon just pinching that knuckle will make you feel great and you won't have the faintest idea why!

Who's up for feeling good for no reason – at will?

Finally, let your spirit run free! (That, after all, is a core message of this book). Experiment a little. Or a lot. If you have a bad day, try turning the images of things that have happened into cartoons, or spin them around like a "headline" in an old movie – only spin them *away* from yourself. Change the colours to black and white. Have Scooby-Doo show up and scare things away ... just *play*.

The net effect you're after is to get yourself to fully accept that *you* are master of your feelings - not outside influences. As you go through the book you will understand at a much deeper level that life is *responding* to you and not *happening* to you. But I admit the illusion that it is all "them" and nothing to do with "me" is sometimes still a persuasive one, especially when looking at the issue from your end means accepting an uncomfortable home truth or two.

The more you do it, the more in control you'll become. And what I've discovered is that it's mostly self-control and not knowledge that truly gives you power over your life and your destiny.

# 10: What Do You REALLY Want?

When you were a child, say around six or seven years old up to the age of, oh I don't know, let us say seventeen to twenty, what did you *really* want?

When grown ups, (maybe should read *groan*-ups), asked you that oh-so dull question, "And what do you want to be when you grow up?" what went through your mind? (Apart from, "I wish you'd stop asking me that dumb question," of course!)

I can only hazard a totally random guess, since obviously I know very little about you – not even your gender or age. But I do know that you're searching for something or you wouldn't be reading a book such as this one.

Perhaps you wanted to change the world or just to see most of it. Maybe you dreamed of pop stardom, acting or happy marriage and gorgeous kids – or all of the above. Some of you may have wanted to take the medical or scientific worlds by storm, others wanted to excel at some sport ... the list is clearly potentially endless.

Here, however, is what I can practically guarantee you did *not* dream:

You didn't want to live on State benefit in a run down area of town. You never expected to have to worry about paying bills or driving a beaten up second hand car. No one dreams of becoming a criminal or a victim of crime. You didn't dream of being divorced, heartbroken or lonely. You didn't dream of becoming addicted to anything or of feeling you had no choice but to work in a humdrum job that barely makes ends meet and which to all intents and purposes, you hate.

I know that's bleak, and there's a reasonable chance that you personally are somewhere between the two extremes I've depicted there. But millions of people in the so called first world live on or below the kind of poverty line I described above. Indeed, I have met inhabitants of third world countries who live with fewer resources, and certainly no State help, but who are far happier than many of the Western people I know.

I also know that if there are more people living in ways they'd rather not that I have begged the question, "If we can create our own reality, how come there's so much poverty, disease and misery about?"

The answer(s) to that very important question will become clear as you go through the book. It is absolutely not my intention to dodge it – it's a key issue, and understanding the answer will not only lift you to a place where it can't and won't ever happen to you, but it will also enable you to inspire and help others.

For now, the short and less than adequate answer is that the people who live in misery mostly do not know or believe that they have any choice. And please note that many people who live in third world countries in conditions which most of us in the wealthy West cannot imagine, are not all unhappy by a long chalk.

Many are, I agree, but for all and any who suffer anywhere I will, for now, say only this: You cannot help them by becoming one of them. You can never get miserable enough to lift someone out of depression, or sick enough to heal someone or poor enough to shift people out of poverty. It only takes one candle flame to eliminate all the darkness in a room and you must *become* that candle flame if you are going to help in any way.

## *What About Your Dreams?*

The question we must address first and foremost, however, is "What happened to your dreams?"

When did you switch them off?

Why did you do that?

When did you decide that "being realistic" was synonymous with giving up on your most cherished and exciting passions?

In the "Do-Have-Be" model we've been indoctrinated with, here's what "realistic" looks like:

- Work hard at school/college/university and get good grades. (Even in subjects you don't care about.)
- Use those grades to beat your fellow graduates to a "decent" job. This proves your worth and also means you can hold your head high whilst seeking out a mate.
- Find the mate and procreate. Along the way, accrue considerable debt, most of it on a "nice" house that family, friends and neighbours will admire. You can add to this burden with a car and credit cards, some of which

you can spend on holidays in places you and your family couldn't otherwise afford.

- Keep going for around forty years, (or longer). At some point, some of the debts will – if you're lucky – fade away and you will receive a pension to keep you in your fading years which, in most cases, is not going to be enough to do more than survive – i.e. pay the bills and groceries, and so any dreams that you may have had are finally put to bed.

- Meanwhile, hope your kids find a way to live theirs, but don't build up their hopes too much because you know how much it hurts when you fall.

Now here's how that version of "realistic" feels:

- *Disappointing!*

Is that all life is for? Drudgery, debt payment and dreaming things that are so far out of reach you wonder why God gave you an imagination in the first place? Isn't that all a waste of everyone's time?

Phew! I don't like that picture at all. Let's rewind. Let's go back to the question of what you really dreamed of when you were young. (You're still young if you're still dreaming! The number of birthdays you've had is irrelevant!)

So, what *did* you dream?

I've already pointed out that I can't even hazard a guess at the answer, so I suggest you pause at this point and pull out a notebook and pen, and maybe a box of tissues, (this can get emotional), and write down everything you can remember about that. Don't hold back – what did you really, really want to do with your life? And what would you really, really want to do with it now?

Remember, I said don't hold back. Go ahead. I'll wait for you.

Great. Now keep those notes for later – you'll want to refer back to them.

Here is how "realistic" looks in the "Be-Do-Have" model. This applies in any and every field of human endeavour you can name:

- I set exciting goals that turn me on and I easily get most of them.
- Those I don't get I enjoy going after.
- I believe I can achieve anything I set my mind and heart on.
- I love my life.
- I'm popular and inspirational to others.

(There maybe more, but you've got the idea).

Now, here's the killer question: What makes the difference between those folks and the rest of the dreamers? How come they made it?

You don't have to be rich and/or famous to have a life with those characteristics. But we'll have to refer to a few rich and famous folks because they're the ones everybody's heard of!

One of the biographies that inspires me most is that of an American woman. See if you know who she is:

She was born to a negro mother so poor that she sometimes dressed her in grocery sacks. This was also during a period when racism was rife in parts of the USA.

She never knew her father.

She was physically and sexually abused throughout her childhood.

She became a "delinquent" as a teenager and got in trouble with the law.

She was raped when still a teenager which resulted in a stillborn infant.

A judge said that she would spend her life, which he also predicted would be very short, in institutions.

Do you know who I'm talking about?

This is *Oprah Winfrey*. Now, Oprah may be an *institution*, but she is certainly also one of the most highly respected and influential women in the world. She is most certainly an *inspiration*.

No one can ever say of Oprah, "Yeah, but look at all the opportunities *she* had…" Oprah had less than nothing!

No matter how you analyse it or try to excuse it, there are people from all walks of life and cultures, of all ages, of both genders, of all colours, creeds and backgrounds who have achieved incredible things in any area of human endeavour you care to name.

Henry Ford was considered close to *insane* by his backers, friends and family when he said he wanted to mass produce the motor car. He was told that it could not be done and that no one would want cars on a mass scale!

(He actually told his engineers to come up with a way of putting all four cylinders into a single engine block which they told Henry was impossible. Henry's response? "Do it anyway!")

Sylvester Stallone was turned away by agent after agent. Everyone told him he could not act – they even said he was too ugly! He reached a point where he could not afford to heat his home – and this was New York in winter – so he spent his days in the warm library where he wrote the screenplay for Rocky!

The rest is history. Well, almost. The agents liked the script but didn't want Stallone in the movie. Despite being desperately poor, Stallone refused to sell them the script unless he was allowed to star in the film.

By now so poor that he could hardly afford to eat, he gave away his best and most loyal friend – his dog – to a lonely stranger he met outside a liquor store. He never even asked the man's name, but he did ensure that he was just lonely and not a drunk before handing over the dog.

Eventually, an agency made him a pittance offer to make and star in Rocky, which included a percentage of takings. The agency thought that Stallone would never collect as the movie would never be anything more than a forgotten "B" movie. Stallone agreed, and with the small amount of money he was given up front, went to find the new owner of his dog and buy him back!

After several long evenings of waiting outside the liquor store the man and dog appeared. Stallone offered to buy the dog back, but the guy wasn't selling. Eventually the two men struck up a deal. The guy agreed to give the dog back if both he and the animal could have a part in the movie. Stallone agreed, and they can both be seen in the film!

Inspired or stupid? Determined or daft? Stallone almost wrecked his marriage with his stubborn pursuit of his dream, and I've never met Mr. Stallone so I've never asked him about that period of his life, but I suspect that he would say that there simply was nothing else to do with his life. That is what he is here to do – to act and entertain.

Billy Joel came close to suicide when he thought that no one wanted his music. Perhaps, had he been armed with some of the knowledge that you will have once you've read this book, he might not have gone to such a dark place, but the point is that these folks see no point in life if they cannot live their dreams.

Weren't these people using "struggle & effort" to break through to the successes they respectively desired? I hear your cry. But no, I don't believe they were. Whenever they followed their passions *they felt good*. Sylvester Stallone could unquestionably have got a day job and paid his heating bills, and doubtless made the atmosphere between himself and his wife a lot sweeter too!

But he would have felt *terrible*. Living in a way that feels terrible all the time *is* struggle and effort and it causes more struggle and effort as we endeavour, against the calling of our hearts and souls, to keep it all going. That's *stress* and it is literally and figuratively a *killer*.

I don't believe for one second that this is stubborn stupidity. I think it is the calling of their souls. Now, most of us don't go to the extremes that Stallone or Joel did, and neither do we endure, for the most part, the traumas and suffering that Oprah experienced. We do something far worse.

We *bury* the calling of our souls!

Now it is time to reawaken them. Because there are no reasons or excuses why you cannot turn them all into reality. You can shape and drive your own destiny. You can design it and whilst it's being delivered you can enjoy the journey and gleefully anticipate the change in fortunes that's coming your way as surely as a child knows that Santa will be coming down the chimney next December 24th.

# 11: I Didn't Mean To Ask God, But He Turned Out Quite Helpful!

I was not brought up religious. My mother, until the last twenty four months of her life, thought that all religion was just so much claptrap. She was, however, born to a Jewish family which qualified her in my father's eyes, (amongst other attributes it must be said), to be his wife. Not being Jewish would have disqualified her regardless of how wonderful she was in other ways!

My father, by the time I entered the world in 1956, had dropped most of the rituals expected of an orthodox Jew. Being married to my mother, I suspect may have had a little to do with that, but my father's own character was such that he preferred to study the wisdom underlying religious teachings.

He therefore steeped himself in Theosophy, (too complex for me to this day), the Kabala and Buddhist ideologies as well as the hidden meanings in Hebrew scrolls and so on. My father was drawn to the *intellectual* aspects of religion.

I was aware of things that I suspect most of my English or even Jewish contemporaries were not aware of by the age of five or six. I had heard of the Buddhist eight-fold path, (though I couldn't tell you what it was), I had learned that this world is sometimes called *maya* (or illusion), although it felt real enough to me, and I could tell you that *nirvana* was a heavenly state to be attained but ideally not desired, since Buddhism says that desire is the root of all suffering.

I didn't *understand* a word of it.

But I could sound good at a grown ups' tea party!

The message that I did somehow absorb from living and growing up in this eclectic culture was that you didn't have to take what came your way at face value. It was okay to ask what life meant and what it was for.

That much I did understand, and that proved to be most useful as it turned out.

When, unbeknown to me, my mother was diagnosed with breast cancer at the age of just thirty-eight, she "found" a religious book amongst my father's comprehensive personal library. She thought it was a book on health, a subject even closer to her heart at that time than at any other, although she had always had a keen interest in staying healthy, ironic though that may sound.

The book was "Science and Health with Key to the Scriptures." My mother thought she wouldn't be interested in the scriptures part and intended to explore the chapters on health and science. However, the book, as you may know, is written by Mary Baker Eddy who is the founder of Christian Science – a deeply religious movement.

To my mother's own astonishment, she found great comfort in this book and for the next couple of years we had a lot of Christian Scientist friends and healers around us. They have a particular way of praying, which I confess I have long forgotten, but a kindly lady did teach me at the time, (I would have been seven or eight years old), and which my mother encouraged me to practice, admitting that it seemed odd even to her to be asking such a thing. But it felt right and so we did it.

I had not been allowed to know my mother's diagnosis – such was her own wish. There came a night in early 1966 when I went to kiss my now virtually bedridden mother goodnight, and I found her dabbing her eyes. As I kissed her she told me to pray for her.

This was the first and only time she had ever asked for such a thing and I knew it was very, very serious.

So I went to bed and prayed with all my might for my mother and at 4.a.m. the next morning my father woke me to say she had died.

I instantly abandoned all and any idea of God. I decided without any need for a single further thought that He didn't exist.

And in a sense, I was right.

Fast forward twenty years. I had a respectable and very interesting job in the Health Service, I had just bought my first home, (so I was strapped for cash), and I was still single.

Being single started to rankle. One by one my friends had married and since I was approaching thirty I somehow began to wonder if there was something the matter with me! I wasn't desperate to marry, especially as I didn't even have a girlfriend at the time, but I was certainly open to meeting someone special.

Now, you should understand that my father's attitude to esoteric knowledge had rubbed off on me. To this day I read voraciously, especially books on spirituality and the areas where new science is at last catching up with ancient wisdom. In those days it was more self help and therapy topics that attracted my attention.

I had gotten hold of a book whose title I believe was "When All You've Ever Wanted Isn't Enough."Error: Reference source not found The title alone had sold it to me. I'd never heard of the author, but it was a slim paperback and I was open to consuming and appraising his ideas. This is important, because I bought the book without really scrutinising it too much. Had I done so I would certainly have rejected it and life would have been very different.

The reason I would have rejected it is because the author, whose name was printed on the cover simply as "Harold Kushner" turned out to be "Rabbi Harold Kushner" – a fact which would have instantly persuaded me that the book was out to preach me religion and I, as you now know, hadn't the remotest interest in that.

But by the time Harold mentioned his association with the cloth I was hooked.

I long ago lost my copy of that book but the lesson I learned from it – and the subsequent experience that lesson gave me – I have never forgotten, nor shall I.

Kushner, referring to the tale of Ecclesiastes if memory serves, was considering the Biblical God. He explained that God was either depicted as omnipotent, (all powerful), or as "all loving."

This bright man then went onto say that if God was indeed omnipotent he was something of a despot since he let innocent people die whilst villains marched on unimpeded. (Forgive me, Rabbi, I am paraphrasing – I no longer have your book, but this is how I remember your argument a quarter of a century after reading it!)

Kushner then examined the possibility of an all loving God and once again pointed out that any "parent" (as in God the Father), who let his children suffer in any of the myriad forms of suffering we see on this planet would be reported to the authorities! No one could call such a father "loving"!

Wow! Here was a man of the cloth tearing into the Biblical depiction of God himself. Now it became paramount to me that Kushner was a Rabbi as I kept turning the pages because I assumed that any atheist would use those arguments to conclude that God did not exist. But since Kushner was, so far as I could tell, still ministering to his flock I couldn't see how he could draw such a conclusion.

I was right, because Rabbi Kushner's conclusion opened my eyes to a way of viewing and considering God that shook me to my very roots and changed my life, quite literally forever.

He said that perhaps God wasn't out there judging or making decisions. He wasn't giving cancer to some and taking it away from others. Maybe, he said, God was just the designer, the architect, who put it all together but who never intended to keep checking every cog and gear.

What use, then, was God to us mortals, if any? Kushner, you'll be glad to know, did not shy away from this question.

Suppose, he suggested, that you are driving home and you see a plume of smoke rising into the sky. You realise a building is on fire and it could be in your street. Kushner said that it would be no use sitting at the lights praying, "Please God, don't let that be my house on fire." Because if your house was the one on fire the flames would not go out or leap to the house next door!

Instead, he reasons, you could ask, "Dear God, whatever that is, give me the strength, courage and resources I need to cope with it."

Now *that* I could deal with! Suddenly it struck me like a thunderbolt that twenty years previously I could have prayed, "Dear God, whatever happens to my Mummy, help us all to cope with it…"

I could have lived with that.

Kushner's argument didn't convince me, but it made me think about God for the first time in my adult life..

A few weeks after reading this I arrived home from work one November night. It was cold and I needed to be frugal with heating. My friends – most of them married – were all busy. There was nothing on TV I wanted to watch and it seemed like a long time till morning.

In my heart, I knew I had nothing to complain about. I had a great job, fantastic colleagues and now a brand new home I could call my own – but the loneliness was starting to eat me up. I was, I can now see, a shining example of having *done* lots of hard work to *have* lots of stuff, but I had forgotten – or rather not yet realised – to *be* happy first!

I flung my overcoat on a chair because I couldn't be bothered to hang it up and flopped onto my sofa. I closed my eyes and tried to think of ways to fill the empty hours until morning. It was whilst in this semi-dreamy state that I started thinking about Kushner's book.

Then I did something that, at the time, had anyone known, I would have felt more embarrassed about than if I'd walked naked through Trafalgar Square at rush hour. I *prayed*.

I did it silently of course. In my mind I simply said, "Okay. I don't really believe in you and my house is not on fire, but I'm lonely. Please give me the resources to cope."

I rather liked the "resources to cope" strategy because it wasn't like asking for a girlfriend to appear out of nowhere, although I have, in more whimsical moments, wondered if one might have appeared had I asked!

I did not expect an answer of course. Indeed I believed there was no answer, and had there been one I would surely have thought of it. After all, there was no God to think of one, was there? There was, in my belief system, only me.

I remained with my eyes closed on the sofa, hoping I would fall asleep and wake up in time to go to bed. (It was only about 5.30 in the evening).

And then, in my mind's eye I saw a woman's name *spell itself out, letter by letter* as if in neon lights. "E ... L.... L... A." I had *no conscious part in this whatsoever*. At the time I found it rather spooky, but now I can see that the experience was *effortless*.

I didn't know anyone called Ella, so I dismissed it. Well, not unless you counted lovely Ella that I'd briefly dated a couple of years before. *That* Ella was gorgeous and very intelligent. A deep thinking beauty – perfect for a man like me! But Ella had other fish to fry and we'd parted on good terms.

But I wasn't having flashbacks of good times spent with Ella. I was just seeing letters in my head. Perhaps it was an acronym.

It came again, brighter this time – real neon pink. "E …. L …. L …. A." Once more I tried mentally brushing it aside, and once more it returned, insistent and bright.

Only then did I connect what was happening with my prayer!

I sat bolt upright, shaken. The letters meant nothing to me unless they related to Ella, my ex.

I confess I was frightened. If God was indeed answering my little prayer the least I thought I had better do was to listen.

Ella, Ella! What should I do with this information? I'd bumped into her once or twice in the previous couple of years but I wasn't sure if she was still at her old address. Someone once told me they thought she'd married.

Please understand me clearly: I still didn't believe in God. This wasn't an epiphany. But it was unbidden, (consciously), and it was a little *scary*.

I scrabbled through some yet-to-be unpacked boxes and found an old diary with Ella's number in it. I was sure she'd have moved or a gruff sounding husband would answer the phone. But it rang – and she answered!

Stumbling my way through some overdue "Hello's" I managed to explain that I just needed a long chat, (which she was delighted to have), and maybe a drink, (which I thought I'd need but she wasn't available for).

So we spoke on the phone – for hour upon hour – until my heart sang and bedtime arrived unnoticed. I felt *wonderful*.

Ella turned out to be just the tonic I needed and she helped me to see my situation very differently that night.

Or, another way to put that, is that she was the answer to my prayer!

After that, I could never again completely dismiss God as a concept, but I was still loathe to accept a being – or even a representation of a being – who resides somewhere above the clouds making rules and judgement calls on innocent folk and entire planets to boot.

At this point I should reveal a little more about my character. I must have been a precocious child because I asked what I would now think of as astonishing questions.

For example:

"How come there are always enough men and women on the planet for people to keep making babies?"

Ahh! How cute! Yes, maybe it is, coming from the mouth of a five year old. But I *still* marvel at that. I'd been told, (when my mother was expecting my brother I suspect), that you couldn't choose or know whether the baby would be a boy or girl. (This was 1964). And so it was logical, (to me anyway), to deduce that it was *possible* for the world to fill up with all males or all females.

But that never happens – not to any species as far as I'm aware. I'm not an anthropologist so maybe I'm wrong, but I've never heard of extinction being caused by gender imbalance.

Years later, Alan W. Watts, the great interpreter of Eastern philosophies, would make me think about how entire plums, plum trees and even a whole plum orchard can come from a single plum stone less than half the size of my thumb.

He spoke of putting it in the ground and then, "…you watch it and you watch it, and after a while the darned thing just *plums*." "To Plum" – he made it a verb because he rightly saw that everything is a process and not a static thing!

So where did you come from? I'm not talking about "the birds and the bees" here! The biological answer is a cop-out! Knowing the process of procreation does not explain how you, with all your complexities and idiosyncrasies showed up!

In the end, I was forced to consider how things show up in this organised way.

Phil Gosling is a droll and brilliant Yorkshire millionaire who began his professional life as a nuclear physicist, (which, he assures his audiences, was utterly without glamour). He has for some years now made a considerable fortune running businesses on the internet.

But Phil backs up his success with a philosophy surprising for a man steeped in "conventional" science and whose roots are in such a down to earth location. He *knows* without question that he attracts all the good that has happened to him, (and it is not only in material wealth that Phil is successful). And he makes a very interesting point about *volcanic lava*.

Lava, that hot substance spewed out by volcanoes over countless millennia, has all the same ingredients that go into making bicycle frames. And yet, despite those boiling cauldrons and all the activity going on, not a single tube of metal has ever emerged from a volcano!

Yes, I know it makes you smile. But I hope it also makes you *think*. There is an *organising principle* to things. Not only that, but the marvels that do appear on this planet and in this amazing universe, do so *without effort*. That's not the same as doing without activity. I'm not talking about creating worlds from the perspective of a couch potato. On the contrary. Unimaginable energy goes into everything from the manufacture of galaxies to daisies and ants. But it all happens without *struggle*.

Life and death, the changing of the seasons, the exchange of gases when we breathe, the healing of wounds even – it all goes on without effort. Where on earth did we get the idea that to have life turn out the way we want it we have to push and hurt ourselves and others? Who told us that hard work is the route to success and happiness? My own father worked his butt off all his life but he got very little of what he truly wanted from his life, and he is hardly an isolated case!

By now you can see, no doubt, where I am taking this line of argument. Another of my childhood musings went like this:

Cavemen must have wondered where they came from. They couldn't get a clear answer so they thought there must be a power that created them and everything. Eventually, people called that power *God*. So human beings invented God!

Who created whom?

Of course there isn't a separate being or entity! How could there be anything separate? What would have created *that*? Where would it be? If it isn't physical, okay, it doesn't need a place to be, but it must be energy of some kind – very powerful and intelligent energy.

This is the energy that can pull a fruit orchard from a plum stone, or you from two microscopic cells. Or galaxies from nothing!

The energy that gives life *is* life, so it must be everywhere or there would be no life and no consciousness of being alive – no self awareness. If it is everywhere then there is nowhere that it is not.

If there is nowhere that it is not, it must be in you – *and you must be a part of it.*

If God gave us free will, then he wouldn't have made rules! (God could surely have things any way He wanted without having to tell people how to behave like a Dickensian schoolmaster!)

If we have free will, then we must be free to choose how to live – and we must have the power to bring that into being.

We can create what we want first of all in our minds – in our amazing imaginations. (Did anyone ask Darwin why nature gave human beings imaginations? It isn't necessary for survival of the species, is it? There was no "need" to come out of caves – just our ability to imagine new ways of living.)

If we can create what we want in our minds then it doesn't make sense that anything, seen or unseen, would withhold it from us.

Whilst it is clear that each of us, as individuals, cannot create a world or even a daisy, we *do* have immense power to influence circumstances and our reactions to what we perceive. In fact, we can even choose *how* to perceive. (This was the principle on which Fritz Perls created the very powerful Gestalt Therapy).

So we can create our personal reality any way we want it. Don't take that lightly. Contemporary people who have understood this principle include Anthony Robbins, Sir Richard Branson, Oprah Winfrey, Dr. Wayne W. Dyer and many others – all of whom are powerful forces for good in the world and who are changing the lives of *millions* of people for the better.

I have no right to tell you what to believe, but I think that as an author of self help material I have a duty to show you how I arrived – kicking and screaming to begin with – at what I believe because believing it has made all the difference.

Ultimately, you have a choice. You already have seen that you have a choice about what you think, focus upon and feel.

You also have a choice, as Einstein pointed out, of deciding on one of the most fundamental questions of all: whether you believe this to be a friendly or a hostile universe.

When I thought I was a product of a random accident, that I was born for a stupidly insignificant amount of time considering how long eternity is, (you're dead a long time!), that this planet had life on it because of a series of improbable accidents and that all that happened to me was a matter of chance, I was struggling, often miserable, frequently lonely, usually on the point of being broke and taking happiness as the odd lucky break along an otherwise treacherous, complex and difficult path.

Having changed my belief system, I feel happy every day with all that I am and all that I have. I am married to one of the happiest women alive who is a sheer delight to know and spend time with. I have money in the bank for almost the first prolonged time in my life. I love everything that I do and more important than any of that, I love being me!

As if that wasn't enough, I know that there is nothing I can't handle. No "problem" is insurmountable or without a solution. In fact, I welcome the challenges of life now because I know they are helping me to define what I *do* want from any given situation, and that once I have got that definition clear, it is only a matter of time, (often very little time), before the desired outcome shows up.

My hope is, as a reader of my book so far, that you will at least open your mind to the possibility that a belief system similar to mine may bring you the relief you have been seeking too.

After all, the worst that can happen is that you feel good a lot of the time.

Does God exist, then? To my mind Kushner's God does, yes. The tyrannical, angry, jealous and judgmental God of the Bible and other holy texts makes no sense to me. As Kushner pointed out, if such a God does exist, I would certainly not be praying to him!

You decide. You will decide because you *can*. And that is one of your amazing God-given powers! What is more, because you are a self aware human being who knows there was a time before you were here and there will come a time when you are not here, you cannot *not* wonder about how you – and everything else – got here.

Incidentally, you cannot *not* decide! It would be impossible for a self aware human being, which you are, not to wonder where you came from and how all of this got here.

## *A Word About Meditation*

To some people, I know, meditation seems like mystical hocus-pocus and an excuse for a nap! Merely observing it I can understand why it might seem that way.

There is a story of a journalist who was given a free pass to one of Anthony Robbins' events so that he could report on it. Now, if you've never been to a Tony Robbins event you should know that there are serious echoes of rock'n'roll concerts. There are laser light shows, people stand and dance on their seats, there are sometimes dancers on stage and so on. The events, which last several days, often go on late into the night.

People learn better when they're having fun, and they have a lot more staying power and concentration ability if they aren't stuck frozen in their chairs for hours on end. So Tony has his reasons for providing a high level of entertainment and for getting people to move and laugh and dance.

The journalist was instructed to participate fully. But he didn't. Instead he sat at the back of the room, (which would have had around two thousand people in it), and took notes. He left each day at five o'clock because that was when he finished work!

When his report came out he claimed that it was all a waste of time and his life had not changed a bit!

Meditation is one of those things too that can't be explained. I cannot tell you in a book what it will do for you or what it feels like. That would be like writing the journalist's report on the Tony Robbins event.

I don't want to prescribe meditation; that will only make you resist it anyway. I want you to be *drawn* to try it.

The reason for doing it is because it's a gentle, simple way to stop feeling separate and to have some experience of being connected to everything – what I and others have come to call "source energy."

This is the energy that creates worlds as well as you. It is where ideas and inspiration (= *"in spirit"*) come from. Many of the passages in this book were written after a period of meditation – the ideas just floated into my awareness.

That's wholly different from sitting and *thinking* what to write. I knew where I wanted to take the book – but topics and even how to put them across often would just "come to mind". Even the book's title came to me that way.

But – and this is where I run out of any means to explain it – I can't tell you how that happened. There was no "trying." I didn't begin my meditation period with any *intention* to get ideas. I was holding that intention throughout my daily life anyway.

So ... I hope you can see ... it was when I *let go* of trying to get hold of or to generate ideas, (through meditation), that the ideas were "freed" to float to the surface.

Now, I don't want to give you the impression that meditation is only useful when you want some result, or that I only meditate when I'm being creative. I meditate most days. I mean well over ninety percent of days. And I don't beat myself up on the days I miss either.

Meditation isn't something you can try once and then say you didn't notice any difference. It needs to become part of your daily routine like cleaning your teeth. As Marianne Williamson put it in one of her lectures, you start each day by washing yesterday's dirt off your body, why wouldn't you cleanse your mind too?

The effects, among many other subtle ones I can't think how to name, are that it makes me more peaceful, more resourceful and more creative. It also makes me grateful and it is twenty minutes when I don't just slow down – I can actually stop.

And no, it is *not* the same as watching the football on TV as one gentleman tried to convince me once, and it is not, I assure you, the same as sleep. It a gentle state of awareness – and above all it is *effortless*. It will teach you – over time – the art of effortlessness.

For now, that's enough about why I think you should give meditation a try. As I said, I want you to be drawn to it – it isn't supposed to feel like a chore! I can honestly say that on the days when I don't meditate I genuinely miss it.

If you are going to introduce it into your life, I suggest you be willing to try it for ninety days. You really aren't going to feel or notice much difference in less time than that. And the differences are *subtle*. You have more peace of mind, more resilience, more creativity. Your ego is less sensitive; you discover good in people and things where before you could only see nuisance value or worse.

Open to it? Good for you! There are dozens of methods out there, but here is the simplest I can think of.

## A Simple Way To Meditate.

You need to set aside fifteen minutes a day. Twice a day, morning and evening is recommended by some sources, so decide how much you are interested to put into this experiment.

Sit in a comfortable chair and wear comfortable clothes. There is no requirement to sit in the lotus position! However, don't cross your legs or fold your arms and rest your palms in your lap. You should be able to breathe easily and without anything restricting you.

Ensure there are no phones or other things that can disturb you. Have a watch or clock nearby – but don't set an alarm. (Your subconscious knows how long fifteen minutes feels – and you will be surprised at how accurate it can be!)

Close your eyes and focus on your breathing. You don't need to change your breathing, just be aware of it. As you breathe in, think "Breathing in," and as you breathe out, "Breathing out."

Sounds boring? Yes! As your mind gets bored with that – and it will do so very quickly – it will drift off and try to entertain itself with all sorts of day to day trivia.

As soon as you notice that that's what it's doing, there's no need to beat yourself up – (this isn't a competition!) Simply notice – and then return your awareness to your breathing once more.

Your mind will drift off again in all probability. Gently bring your awareness back to your breathing ...

And so on.

Fifteen minutes. It gets easier, but the key point is to be gentle with yourself! Your chattering mind eventually learns, like a wayward toddler does, to behave itself, but it is unlikely you will ever get all the way through fifteen minutes totally focussed on your breaths. Maybe you will – once in a blue moon. But this isn't a competition. It's a gentle exercise in stillness and allowing. So be gentle with yourself.

However, what you *will* start to experience are moments when you are neither focussing on your breathing nor listening to your chattering mind.

Those moments – which you only become aware of when you "return" – are blissful. Those are the moments when you and Source Energy are one. You aren't asleep – you'll know because it feels different to sleep.

Of course, you can't *make* those moments happen – and you aren't "failing" at meditation if they never happen! The all important thing is the letting go.

And this is the point at which I let go of instructing you in meditation.

# 12: The Power Of Changing Your Mind

No one is born "broken." No tiny infant ever suffered from low self esteem or fretted over a relationship issue. Babies don't worry about the state of the economy or what's in their wardrobe. In short, you are born *whole*. You accept yourself and life, moment by moment, as it is.

The argument then runs that innocence, (which really means "ignorance" in this context), is the reason babies don't have any problems. We become *aware* of the "real" world of responsibilities and challenges as we grow into adulthood and it is only then that our troubles really begin.

In my view this whole argument is a lie. It is a widely perpetuated lie, and one many of us tell to ourselves on a regular basis. I myself bought it for many years. But I do urge you now, as you read these words, to be ready to dismiss it and indeed banish it from ever entering your mind again because it is one of the most evil and pernicious lies ever to be told and it can dominate and ruin your life.

As a member of the human race you came into this life equipped with an extraordinary ability. It is so extraordinary that it allows us to adapt to almost any situation or environment, and to overcome unbelievable adversity. It is also this ability that enables us to achieve great success, feats of endurance, or to invent new things and ideas seemingly out of nothing.

And yet this great ability, perhaps because each and every one of us has it, is almost entirely overlooked, or at best consigned to the "marginally useful" category as if it were of no more importance than being able to flutter your eyelids at will.

I am speaking of the ability to choose what to think about. I am no anthropologist, but as far as I know, no other creature can do this. If they can, it doesn't show in their behaviour or development. But *you* can, and that is what counts.

If I suggest to you now that you can start thinking of elephants then that is precisely what you can do. You may think of elephants you have seen or even met, perhaps on safari, in a zoo or even in the wild. You may think of documentaries you have seen on television about elephants, cartoon elephants, toy elephants, cuddly elephants and so on. But the fact is you can do it to order – no matter what you may have been thinking about a moment before.

Now, it is important that you know something more about this phenomenal ability of yours and how it works. If I now instruct you to *not* think of elephants you will notice an interesting result occurring. So for a few seconds let's experiment with that instruction – don't think of any elephants! Stop thinking of elephants right now! Under no circumstances are you to think of elephants...

What is happening in your head? Well, I'm no mind reader, but there will still be thoughts of elephants in there! You can't help it – and that is an important thing for you to know about your subconscious: it doesn't take "no" for an answer. In fact, it doesn't even understand "no." I have heard the subconscious mind described as a three year old genie. (It could just as easily have been a three year old genius which would have been equally accurate).

A three year old believes whatever you tell it and acts and reacts accordingly. Okay, mostly. But if you give a small child a full glass of milk and add the instruction, "Don't spill it," you have now made the child's head fill with images and ideas of spilling the drink, thus dramatically increasing the likelihood of spillage! "Hold it steady" or something similar would be a much better instruction.

So it is with your subconscious mind. But there's more. Your subconscious also has a perfect "sat-nav" system built in. This means that you can now issue instructions regarding where you want to go, (in life or with a project, love affair … you name it), and your sat-nav will let you know when you're off course. That navigation system is called your emotions!

## *"e"-motions!*

Yes, I know that's not how you spell "emotions" but there's a reason I've put the "e" in quotes and a hyphen in the word.

If you remember your basic Einstein relativity theory, (and who doesn't?), you'll recall that $e=mc^2$. "e" stands for *energy*. Emotions – which are, after all, *moving* experiences are nothing more than *energy in motion*. And when you come to think about it, that's what you are anyway! Energy in motion equals being alive!

(It's okay, you can forget about the rest of Einstein's equation.)

You know when you feel good. Other people know it too – it shows in your face and in your body language. Your whole demeanour will be "sunny" when you're on a high, won't it? You'll have all kinds of words to describe good feelings too, although our vocabulary of emotions is somewhat impoverished for most of us.

Ask your average citizen how they feel on a typical, relatively uneventful day of their life and they'll probably say "okay" or "not bad" – which aren't really descriptions of feelings at all. There is no such emotion as "okay" and I don't know if your feeling okay is anything like mine, do I?

It is actually useful to have a spectrum of words you can use to describe your feelings, and positive ones might therefore include:

Joyful
Happy
Ecstatic.
Excited
Euphoric
Passionate
Wild
Thrilled
Buoyant
Effervescent
Eager
Enthused
Overjoyed
Over the moon

… and a whole lot of slang ones that each generation of teenagers will produce! In the 1980s it became popular for the word "wicked" to be used to mean that something was very good or desirable, whereas I grew up in an age when "wicked" was usually the way evil witches were described in fairy stories such as "The Wizard of Oz."

Although we'll never be precise in terms of comparing your experience with anyone else's, you'll discover that your own experience of life will be enhanced when you have a wider vocabulary of emotion at your disposal. Without it, it's as if you had to describe everything you see in terms of how grey or ungrey something is! Imagine trying to tell someone about a gorgeous sunset by saying, "There was almost no grey anywhere in it!"

By contrast, when you feel bad, you probably already have a wide vocabulary available to you, some of which may not make family reading anyway! What's interesting to note about that is that many of us are far better at noticing when we're off centre or off colour, (there's two expressions straight away!), than we are at being aware of the good times and good things in life.

One result of that skewed view is that when you review your life you tend to talk about your troubles and how this, that or the other didn't work out for you, because that's what you've been trained to remember!

It's as if a car driver would say, "It's typical! The lights always turn red just as I show up!" This is statistically highly unlikely as I'm sure you'd agree. Over the years of motoring, on average lights are going to be green or red about fifty percent of the time respectively when any individual driver shows up at them, aren't they?

This is cultural conditioning, not our natural state! The impression that good things and good times are rare pervades our lives. Listen to any casual conversation between colleagues or friends meeting up on a Monday morning. Just notice what percentage of what they talk about relates to problems, worries and other negatively charged fare.

Rarely do you hear people telling one another how wonderful their lives are. Okay, they might say they saw a great movie or concert – a highlight – but when did you last hear one man tell another how much he appreciates his wife, (or women say the same of their husbands)? When was the last time you told anyone how much you love your home or your neighbourhood, or how much you love waking each day feeling healthy?

Often, we don't even notice these things unless they are threatened in some way. We are groomed and conditioned to think and feel in the negative, and whilst this may make positive things and events stand out in sharper relief, it hardly makes for a great life!

Imagine for a moment if you could reverse this. The news would be full of wonderful, joyous things and your life would be an expression of your passion for each and every moment fully lived. Occasionally there would be a blip and then office chit-chat might sound something like this:

"You'll never guess what happened to me at the weekend! One of my kids was sick for a whole hour! She's fine of course now …"

Mostly, however, it would be more like this:

"My weekend was fabulous thanks. The whole family went to the park and we just spent a couple of hours laughing and playing ball. Isn't it amazing how much fun you can get from a plastic sphere? There'll be so many treasured memories for all of us, and I'm sure the kids will add those moments to their growing portfolio of happy childhood memories.

"Then we all savoured an ice cream. It had started to rain by then so we ate it inside a little coffee shop near the park, and we were just joking about how crazy we were to eat ice cream in the rain…"

Do you think this is crazy or boring perhaps? If you do, maybe that's because you feel most people wouldn't find that interesting. They'd much rather hear about your problems. Then they can either empathise, ("Oh yes. I know exactly what you mean. Something terrible like that happened to me …"), or sympathise, ("That must have been awful. Are you okay?")

But take a look at what's really happening. Remember, we always want to feel better. So the empathiser tries to feel better by turning the tables to see if they can get *you* to care about *their* troubles. At the very least they reinforce a bond of friendship based on mutual misery – and this becomes the token by which you both accept and acknowledge one another. Breaking such bonds can be extraordinarily difficult and mostly we will sink to their level of misery rather than bring people up to our raised bar! The desire to be liked and accepted by our peers is an astonishingly powerful, and much under-noticed phenomenon.

The sympathiser, on the other hand, shows "care" and thus feels needed. In both cases the two of you are creating a relationship based on a phenomenon known as "co-dependency" in which both parties "require" the other to remain in some way off balance – perhaps even "broken" in some way. This is often seen in couples as well as relationships between parents and "difficult" teenagers. In the latter example, the co-dependency is sometimes very easy to spot, with the teenager going off the rails in some way, (drugs, violence, prostitution, petty crime or some form of extreme rebellion), whilst the doting parent appears to attempt to change the behaviour, and consciously believes she wants to.

The truth, however, is often that without a "child" to "care" for the mother, (it is usually but by no means always the mother), would have no role in the family. Subconsciously, she needs her child to be difficult or sick. The child, on the other hand, senses that he cannot abandon his mother to perhaps an abusive or neglectful husband or to a lonely life, so he subconsciously protects her from such a fate by finding ways of being needy.

The point of all this is simple you'll be pleased to know. The point is you can *choose* what to focus on.

I've said it before, and I'll say it again – this is the most incredible power. Don't dismiss it or take it for granted just because anyone can do it.

Consider one of life's most painful events: heartbreak. You can focus on how terrible that is and how your life is over if you wish. That might be appropriate for a short time, although your actual life is clearly not over. But six months, a year or a decade later you are simply giving your life away to someone – your ex - who has almost certainly moved on.

No one is going to feel better by you remaining in that state.

Pain hurts – that's why it's painful. I'm not saying we could or should eliminate pain. Some events are outside of your control anyway. You can't control the forces of nature or the behaviour of other people. (They'll hurt you or leave you if you try!) But you always, *always* have control of your thoughts. Where your mind goes is up to you.

So, in the case of a broken heart for example, once you've had a short time to get over the initial shock, you can start to ask yourself what you can learn. What can you change about yourself? How can you grow? Who can help and support you to do that? The one I asked myself was, "How can I start to enjoy getting to know myself better?" That was a life-saver and a life-changer!

## Negative Emotions Are Not Bad Things

In the "olden days" I grew up in, we used to copy music onto something called cassette tapes. They were useful things in that you could copy your friends' albums and play music in your car, but they had their down sides. One of these was that if the music had sudden crescendos or loud passages the tape would horribly distort the sound.

Some clever tape recorders were then fitted with anti-distortion devices. You could select this technology during the recording process at the push of an extra button. (Don't ask me what they did – I neither know nor care!)

A technically minded friend told me that the device somehow evened out the sound waves so that the tops or bottoms of big changes in the sound were flattened out. The result was less distortion, but also less *contrast*. Big crescendos would lose their punch, whilst the quiet passages would be boosted up a notch.

When I joined the psychiatric health service I learned about a very popular drug called "Valium" – which, as you may well know, still is very much on the market today. As I began to understand a little about what it did and met many patients who were prescribed it, I saw a parallel with the anti-distortion devices used for cassette tapes.

The drug *took the edge off emotions*. People's moods were flattened out. They could feel anxious less easily, but they could feel joyful less easily too! They weren't exactly zombies; I'm not saying that, but they weren't able to focus so well on what they wanted from life either.

They only knew they wanted to not feel so bad, (also a highly subjective term of course, since each of us will have a different threshold for what we feel we can or cannot cope with). I never heard one of those patients say that anyone had explored with them what would make them feel good, nor did anyone demonstrate to them how they could have so easily lifted their own mood.

In other words, self empowerment was not considered. Not surprisingly, many people became psychologically and physically dependent on those pills. There are still many people in that position today.

Let's get one thing really clear. Negative emotions are not bad things. They aren't there to be vanquished like an evil beast, and neither is life meant to be without its ups and downs.

Imagine booking yourself on what has been billed as the most exciting roller coaster ride ever and when you got there you found it was just a train that hurtled along a perfectly flat, straight track. You might well ask for your money back!

But the owners of the ride might argue that they didn't want to shock anyone or make them feel afraid and that after a lot of research a flat track was the best way they could think of to achieve that. In fact, they might tell you, they were even thinking of slowing the ride right down because some people were a little frightened by high speed.

You can see that this is daft if you think about a rollercoaster. But it's how you have been taught to expect life to be! We have almost come to expect as a right that everything should go our way. It is never supposed to rain on our particular parade!

So let's get clear about why negative emotion is a good thing.

Negative emotion is a good thing because it throws into sharp relief what you want. If you never got a sharp kick up your backside there's a distinct possibility you might spend your life sitting upon it!

We *need* contrast. At the simplest of levels we need polarity – which is just another way of saying the same thing. We could have no concept of "down" if everything was "up." Imagine if everything was white, weightless and silent!

When you have a negative emotion, (or to put it in common parlance, when you feel bad), it's a sign that you want to feel good! D'uh! But if you continually focus on how bad you feel you will simply succeed in fanning the flames of the bad feeling and increase it.

The simplest and fastest way out of this trap is to give the bad feeling a name and then ask yourself what feeling you'd like to have instead. So let's go back to my example of heartbreak which, on the face of it, looks like a tough cookie because you feel as though the remedy depends on another person.

So let's say you call the feeling, this worst feeling in the world of feelings, "rejected." You'll have a whole bunch of emotions mixed up in there, but let's work with one at a time.

Next, you ask yourself what feeling you want, and the answer will pop back that you want to feel "accepted and loved by X" – whoever you perceive as having broken your heart, of course.

Now, X isn't coming back, so you have to reconsider your answer. You want to feel accepted and loved.

Right now, you can't think of a remedy for that, so you notice how you feel in *this* moment – and that might be "frustrated and angry."

Rinse and repeat: what emotion would you like *instead* of "frustrated and angry?"

Well, you'd like, let us say, to feel calm and at peace with how things are.

That's still tricky, but we're getting closer. When you try feeling calm and at peace you might notice that what comes up is a lot of sadness. You might well cry at this point. Goody! That's healing and *moving* you too.

And what do you want instead of sadness? The answer may be something very simple like "time out." It might be "happiness" of course and when you reach for that you'll notice another emotion that gets in the way of you getting there now, which might even be anger.

Just keep climbing the emotional ladder in this way. At each step, use your state management skills to put yourself in the appropriate physiology. So, as an example, when you felt "frustrated and angry" when what you wanted was to feel "accepted and loved" – put yourself in the "frustrated and angry" physiology. Go for the one you *can* reach, not the out-of-reach emotion! That would just make you more frustrated and angry.

You don't need to hold any state for more than a few seconds – maybe a minute or two at most. What you'll notice as you climb this ladder is that each "rung" feels a little better than the one before.

With something as powerful as heartbreak it can be a game of "snakes and ladders" too, but doing exercises like this one instils the message that you are in control and not at the mercy of your emotions. I don't mean "control of emotions" in the sense of the British "stiff upper lip" where we suppress and even deny that we're feeling anything. This is quite the opposite – this is about choice!

As time moves on and the initial shock stage passes, you can begin to picture what kind of situation goes with each desired emotion. What would your life look like, for instance, if you were calm and at peace? What would you be doing? Where would you be doing it?

This is too much at the beginning, because every visualisation will include the person who is no longer in your life and will knock you back down the ladder again. Don't worry too much if that happens – you can climb back up, but the aim is to get as close to the top as possible without too many emotional bruises of course!

Incidentally, at the very top of the ladder is total self empowerment, joyful living and complete peace of mind. Does that sound good to you?

The "rungs" I've suggested in the example above, however, are just that – suggestions. Go with what naturally comes up for you.

I want you to get the point that your mind is flexible and that you can control it. I know I'm labouring the point but that is because your mind, which is far more powerful than most of us have yet realised, is the one thing you are always in control of – and that is all you'll ever need to have a happy, fulfilling and wonderful life!

## *The Secret Of Getting Anything You Want*

You don't need to manipulate people to get what you want from them or from life. People will happily fall over themselves to help you and even love you when you're good to them. The secret of getting, if you want to know, is *giving*.

Here's how that works. When you make someone feel good, it feels good to you too. That makes you want to go and make more people feel good and they, in turn, begin making others feel good. The more people they can make feel good the more …

I'm sure you don't need me to go on with that. It's hardly rocket science is it? But what most people fail to realise is that to start the ball rolling they need to feel good in the first place. Then they've got something they can pass on.

Oh, excuse me! I didn't make that quite clear. Let me try again.

**What most people fail to realise is that to start the ball rolling they can CHOOSE to feel good in the first place ... no matter what!**

The more you can do that – that is, make it your way of life and not simply a good idea that you remember for brief moments between bouts of misery, stress, strife, worry, anxiety, frustration, anger, sickness and other forms of debilitation – the more you will have a *fabulous* and *fulfilling* life.

Happiness is all you've ever wanted. I know that because it's all anyone ever wants. Your definition of happiness will have variations on the other six or seven billion that exist currently on this little planet of ours because no two people want precisely the same things.

The key to having it, however, is to really *really* understand that happiness is not the result of acquiring things or status. It doesn't suddenly blossom *after* you find true love. It doesn't come along with promotion or retirement or vacations. In fact it doesn't come *to* you at all. It comes *from* you. Once you know that, access that and live from that one simple truth all that you desire will flow to you effortlessly. That's a promise.

Keep reading! Because if you're anything like most of the rest of us, (myself very much included), you will forget quickly and often about the power you have. Or you will forget to use it. Or both.

Besides that, I know perfectly well that if you are going to believe what I'm telling you the first thing I'm going to have to do is to give you the *experience* that you do indeed possess the power I've been telling about.

Sometimes the results are both rapid and miraculous. I can't promise those, but I can promise that the journey is fun, fulfilling and fabulous.

Prepare to be convinced. Above all, prepare to be *happy*!

# 13: Your Power To Create Reality Effortlessly

We've talked about decisions and changing your mind and the power to choose what you focus on. You've learned that you can consciously switch to a different state of mind instantly and that you can bring good feelings to bear on unwanted responses and change those responses.

That's a lot of power.

A lot.

So now let's put it all together.

The joy of this approach is that it requires no effort, (other than reading through and understanding and then, of course, trying out the ideas.) But this is far from the "effort and struggle method" where you grit your teeth and keep your head down, your nose firmly to the grindstone, (imagine how painful *that* would be), while your back gets a hunch and you get exhausted, frustrated and resentful. Then you can show your kids how to live, right?

Furthermore, you don't need to believe in the law of attraction or metaphysics for it to work. You can simply make a few changes in yourself and watch the results shift and change before your very eyes.

This, then, is the heart of the book.

Where we're headed is the heart of *you*.


## *Decisions Are Emotional*


In case this book reaches you in the distant future, I need to tell you about a fictional character from a once famous TV series. His name is Mr. Spock and in the days of Star Trek he was very popular and famous indeed. Supposedly from the planet Vulcan, his most famous characteristic was that he, in common with his species, was entirely logical. Human emotions he saw as a weakness and a vulnerability.

We like to think of ourselves as logical, but in fact we are not. Sure, we have a logic faculty, but it isn't the way we conduct our lives. Logic, whether we like to think so or not, plays second fiddle to our emotions.

Think of fashion. Any reasonably warm piece of sack would do for clothing in that it would be functional, but we are far more complex than that! I have been known to tease my wife when she buys yet another handbag. I tell her I have only one wallet to keep my personal possessions in. But I know, of course, that for her the bag is not functional – it's a fashion accessory and when she carries it and wears clothes that go with it, she feels great. The manufacturers of those bags know that too!

Of course, I am a victim of fashion too, although mine tends to be more with gadgets and other "boys toys" such as my car. I thought I'd better confess so you know I'm not picking on my lovely wife or indeed women!

Even the house you live in, if you had any say in it, was chosen with emotion. Just check out whether the word "house" and the word "home" have different emotional charges for you. When you've finished your day's work I bet you say, "I'm going home" and never, "I'm going to my house!"

If you've ever been through the process of house-hunting you probably began with a list of very pragmatic considerations. Your budget would have been close to the top, and you would have thought about where you want to live, what kind of dwelling you prefer, amenities you want to have handy and so on.

And then you start looking. The estate agent pulls out all the stops and shows you building after building, but they're never quite right. For some inexplicable reason you just don't feel you could settle in any of them. You may even have got to the stage of wondering if there was something wrong with you, or whether subconsciously you didn't really want to move house.

Out of the blue you find it! Cobweb Cottage, ramshackle, out of town and rather over your budget but you fall instantly in *love* with it. You just *know* you could be happy there forever!

I know that's a rather romanticised and generalised version of the story, but hopefully you can identify with some elements of it. The decision gets made by your *heart* not your head!

Once that's done, your head – the logical aspect of you – can start figuring out the *how* of making it happen. That is where your willpower comes into its own. Willpower, as I've told you before, isn't intended to be used to *stop* yourself from having things your heart desires, its use is in bringing your heart's desires into your world.

Take a moment to reflect on what are the biggest decisions you make, you know, the real life changing ones. You'll doubtless include getting married – or divorced, whether to have or not have children, and buying a home. You might also think of accepting or rejecting some belief system such as an orthodox religion, voluntarily choosing any kind of lifestyle or diet such as vegetarianism for example. Probably you'll add in your career choice and any education you opted for after compulsory schooling was over. We could go on indefinitely with the list. You could even write them down if you like.

Now tiptoe back through that list. Is there honestly any one that you can say was made, or is sustained, on logic alone? (I have had vegetarians *passionately* argue with me that it is not logical to kill animals. The irony is, they seem to get very emotional when putting this argument forward. Me – I'm not standing in judgement either way, okay?)

Imagine picking your life partner logically! You'd say, "I want someone with a good gene pool. She must be under the age of …" You get the picture! It's quite likely, if you are in a permanent relationship that at least one of you silently or loudly exclaimed, "Phwoar!" when you first clapped eyes on the other! That isn't even a word! (My spell checker wants me to change it now! But it functions entirely on logic).

The reason for labouring this point and indeed for writing this chapter if not the entire book is hugely important. The message I'm putting across here flies in the face of what you're probably used to. That's because you have almost certainly been conditioned to let your head rule your decisions.

I'm aware that some readers might even consider what I'm saying here to be irresponsible or even dangerous advice, but that is going to depend on what you consider responsible and safe. And it depends on what you want from your life.

If you are a dealer on the stock exchange you're going to say that you must make your decisions based on a host of logical statistics and probabilities. That may have some truth to it, but I ask you what is the purpose of trading stocks and shares in the first place? To make money, you will tell me.

And the purpose of making money would be what, exactly?

Yes, yes, I know, so that you can have more ... stuff.

And having more stuff ... the purpose of that would be ...?

Oh. It makes you *feel* good!

Losing trades on the stock exchange makes you feel, well, less good. I get that!

Accumulating money for its own sake is patently daft. If you did that on an emotionless and utterly logical basis, well, you wouldn't need much to begin with, would you? Some sack cloth to keep you clothed, a tent or even a cave would keep you dry and perhaps, since you would be living in the twenty first century, you'd prefer to buy your food rather than forage for it. Logically, you'd survive and you wouldn't care if you had nothing else because care is an emotional state.

Of course, I know I've taken that to an extreme but I want to make a point. And the point is: this is your point of power!

# "You Don't Get What You Want – You Get What You ARE."

This is a quote from Dr. Wayne Dyer. He's right. Most of the time we have the tail wagging the dog. We think that we'll *be* happy *when* we get the money … or whatever we perceive ourselves wanting.

But the more unhappy you are the more you will keep your desires away from you. It's said that misery loves company and that's true; the more miserable you are the more miserable people will show up to commiserate with you and you'll just stay in your misery pit!

Happiness also loves company! Optimism and joie de vivre love company. Bright spirited people are never short of company – and opportunities knock on their door with astonishing regularity. *In short, the happier you are, the "luckier" you'll be!*

You can choose in general whether you want to be a giver or a taker in life. Givers get more. Give your time, give your praise, give your gratitude, give a smile or a hug, and of course you can give your material things too including money. However, there is a caveat.

If you give through gritted teeth or give resentfully or give conditionally you are not giving. You are giving in order to get and you may as well just go out with a begging bowl and tell people what you want from them. At least that would be honest!

Giving has to feel good and it has to come from the heart. Think of Christmas times. Are your memories of opening your presents or of the squeals of delight and the joy on the faces of those you gave to? Which of those two types of memory give you the most pleasure to recall?

*Life is forgiving. Not for-getting.*

This is a tough message to get sometimes, so let me help you a little. Start by looking at all you already have. What are you grateful for right now?

I'll share a handful of mine. (If I shared them all I'd fill another book). Out of our bedroom window there is a view of green fields and a rural English village. I *love* that view. One day there was a big rainbow over it and I managed to capture it in a photograph which now hangs on the wall in our home.

Every morning when I get up, rain or shine, in a hurry for work or on a relaxing day, I open the curtains and I breathe in that view. I stand at the window for perhaps ten or twenty seconds and I silently say "thank you" for it. I love its moods. I've seen it bathed in sunshine and I've seen it covered in snow and everything else in between.

That reminds me how grateful I am for my eyesight.

As I head for my shower, I put the radio on and I'm instantly reminded of my love of music. Music makes me happy – or at least a lot of music does, and the radio DJ and the music he plays make me smile. I say another thank you.

Amid all of this, my wife will have kissed me good morning and given me her lovely smile. My wife is a blessing in my life way beyond words. I am loved and cared for and I am very grateful for that and much more about her as you might imagine.

On and on the list goes, and I haven't counted a single "possession" yet. Okay, the radio and my shower are integral to that list, but I hope I am getting across to you that you also will have your very own list of a myriad things to be grateful for.

Feeling good on purpose is easy. You just have to shift your focus a little.

Once you've filled yourself up with your own wealth, (and I haven't mentioned money), now you have a store of things to draw from and you can afford to give some smiles, some thanks to a colleague, a sprinkling of praise and so on.

If you feel down and you're focussed on how to pay your bills there isn't a cat in hell's chance you'll be able to do that! You'll get to the office grumpy and stressed and if you do have a friend there to confide in you'll just talk about how worried you are about your bills.

What can your friend do about that? I doubt he's going to pay them for you, so he can either sympathise, ("Ah, I'm sure it'll be all right. Want a coffee?") or empathise, ("Yeah, I know. We had a huge bill last week. Awful isn't it?")

Now who feels better? Answer: no one. Whose problem is solved? Nobody's. This is a pointless way to carry on, and yet it is happening all over the world as we speak.

The alternative goes something like this: "Good morning! You look great this morning!"

Friend, (slightly taken off guard), "Thanks. I wasn't feeling on top of the world, but you've just cheered me up…"

Now, how do you imagine the day is going to go from there? What did that cost you? Who feels better? *Everyone.*

Is your bill paid? No, but it wasn't anyway. Isn't your boss/someone/something more likely to say, "Hey, I've noticed what a breath of fresh air you are around the place and I'd like to offer you this …(whatever)"?

Startlingly, it doesn't usually happen directly like that. It's as though you throw a rock that causes a ripple in a lake and somewhere half a mile down the bank a little boat is gently rocked by the resulting wave. But the boat couldn't see it coming and from where you are on the bank you can't see the boat or the effect you're having.

The most spectacular result I've had to date was a time when I returned from Hawaii after attending one of Anthony Robbins' seminars. I was "high" from the seminar and I had fallen in love with Hawaii too. But I had scraped my financial barrel dry to get there. When I came back I had an empty bank account and very little work. I couldn't even put petrol in my car for a few days and I was forced to live off what was still left in my depleted larder and the generosity of a couple of friends.

However, I knew that I had a choice. I could either panic and worry or I could stay in my "high." I decided to stay high. Creditors were snapping at my heels and the day for the rent was coming round as the days ticked by. Nothing of note happened for nine scary days.

But I just kept feeling good on purpose and whenever doubt or fear in any form crept in I made myself get back on track emotionally. I had no evidence that anything would change and no reason to even hope. I just kept repeating to myself that something good would come, but that part was tough. The easier "antidote" to the fear and the worry I felt was to keep noticing what I had to be grateful for. I'd just been to *Hawaii* for goodness' sake, so it wasn't hard to conjure up a thousand brilliant memories, but I could have found more "ordinary" things if I'd wanted to.

On the tenth day my phone rang. At the time I was a franchisee for a stop smoking organisation and on the other end of the line was the Irish franchisee – a woman I barely knew. Why would she phone me of all people?

It transpired that she'd managed to get some television exposure on Irish TV for our method and as a result had literally thousands of smokers wanting her help. So many that she was fully booked for the following *two years.* Those appointments had come in just ten days and her phones were still ringing. She needed help fast.

She offered me half the net proceeds over a ten day period – during which time I would see nearly four hundred smokers. (We saw them in groups). I came home with the equivalent of almost nine months' pay – for ten days work!

It was only later I enquired why she had thought to phone me when she didn't really know me and there were many other franchisees she knew quite well. She explained that she wanted someone with high energy and drive and had called only one other franchisee, who, in her view, fitted those criteria. But he wasn't available. He was, however, a friend of mine and had suggested me. When she commented that she didn't know me very well, my friend told her that I'd just come back from the Anthony Robbins event and from that she concluded that I was no slouch and hired me!

In a million years I could not have guessed or foreseen where that change in fortune would come from. You can dismiss it as luck or coincidence – it doesn't really matter and that isn't the point.

The point is how I approached the issue – let's not call it a problem – of having zero funds. I chose to feel good no matter what. And it was on the basis of my *assumed* high energy that I was chosen.

Imagine if I'd allowed myself to feel downhearted and worried for those ten days. How would I have sounded when I answered the phone? Remember, I had no idea who was on the other end of that call, (this was before the days of caller display), and most definitely I had no idea what she was going to say. For all I know, the difference in my tone of voice for the single word, "Hello," had I allowed myself to feel negative could have lost me the deal. The Irish lady was wanting – and would have been tuned into – high energy, passion and stamina.

I have had many other incidents like this since. Most recently, with a car that I'd kept rather beyond its natural life span, I was wondering how I was going to get through another winter with it. I needed a new car. My dream car has for years been a Mercedes Kompressor, and our preference would have been to buy a car outright – we are getting rid of old debts and don't want to take on more.

So I kept a vision of my silver Mercedes in mind and a picture of one on my wall. I repeatedly, (but not obsessively), imagined paying for one and driving it away.

And then some money dropped into my lap. Enough to buy a decent second hand car but I was sure not enough for the dream car. In any case, you don't see many Mercedes Kompressor's on the second hand dealers' forecourts!

The money literally landed unexpectedly in my bank account. My wife and I were out shopping when I "happened" to check my balance in the bank. That alone is something I don't usually do. I know pretty much how much is in the account and I can look it up on line. I just had an urge to go and look on this particular afternoon.

When we found the money we had to try not to dance in the bank, and whooping with glee is apparently not a good idea either, so we restrained ourselves and ran outside.

"I can buy a car!" I exclaimed. We agreed to drive to a big second hand car dealership immediately. As we were looking at the cars – Volkswagen Polo's and Vauxhall Astra's were within my new budget – my wife suddenly shouted, "Here's your dream car, honey!" Sure enough she'd spotted a Mercedes Kompressor C180. We were, however, looking at the back of this beautiful car.

"Wait 'til we see the price ticket," I said, not daring to get my hopes up. Fully expecting to see a price ticket with five digits on it – way out of my reach – I was astonished to see it was no more expensive than the Polo's and Astra's!

Being able to pay cash enabled me to negotiate a good deal and they took my old car for a reasonable price too.

Yes, these are nice – and true stories – and I know that even if I told you a million of them you could still go away shaking your head and muttering, "lucky so-and-so!" I can't convince you otherwise with words.

You, however, can convince yourself by putting this into practice. Your future depends on it, actually. But, as I've said several times already, the worst that can happen is that you get to feel good a lot of the time.

You also get to make other people feel good. Get out of bed each day being grateful and make it your purpose to make as many people feel good all day long in as many ways as you can think of.

Hold your dreams in mind every day too – and watch your life change. Effort is *not* required! This feels great – it's better than ice cream and may even be better than sex! Where's the effort in that?

All you have to do then is *trust* and to do that, just watch the Universe. Will the sun come up tomorrow? Will the Earth keep spinning today? Will your blood cells heal a cut? Is there effort required? Does someone have to remember to wind the Earth up every night to keep it turning? No!

Shift your energy on purpose into good feeling as often as you can and every time you catch yourself drifting back into old patterns.

Your life will change for the better forever. I guarantee it.

# 14: The Power Of Dealing With Your Past

Imagine you're on your first date with someone you've been dying to go out with for ages. There's a restaurant table booked and you're all spruced up. The waiter has taken your order, the candle on the table is lit, soft music is playing and now there is nothing to do until the food arrives but look into one another's eyes.

Your heart is fluttering along with the butterflies in your tummy as your gorgeous date says, "Come on. Tell me about you. I want to know everything there is to know about you…"

And here is what you'll say …

You'll tell her – or him – what you do for a living. You will explain a bit about how and where you grew up and went to school and something brief about your parents and what they were like. You might mention a hobby or two and then you'll shrug and say, "That's about it, really."

Of course you both know there's much, much more. You've been cautious because you want to impress and you don't want to brag but you don't want to sound dull either. Mostly, though, you have been very, very careful not to say anything that might put her – or him – off you!

Had you been at the hospital for an appointment with a specialist you might have given a more specific answer, perhaps about your lifestyle, diet or exercise regime.

The point is, you'll be selective depending on the context. But you'll *always* be selective. It's like when you've had a holiday and you're showing someone the photographs. You don't have a picture of absolutely everything! (Okay, I know *one* guy who does, but no one has a beer with him any more). You select the best views, the funny moments and so on.

With most people, however, when it comes to their life story, they select the parts that they think will help other people to understand *why they are the way they are.*

To illustrate, let's create an extreme example. Suppose someone told you that his mother used to beat him and now he likes to be beaten for kicks, or maybe he is violent himself at home. The "excuse" is, whether spoken or not, "I can't help it because my mother used to beat me."

This is, in fact, absurd. There is no reason whatsoever why someone who was abused has to become abusive, whether to others or themselves. I'm sorry, but I just don't buy that. There are plenty of people who suffered in one way or another in their formative years who have gone on to become very caring and loving and often inspirational men and women.

There is the (probably apocryphal) tale of the man imprisoned for the umpteenth time on some petty crime charge related to his alcohol abuse. In despair, his social worker asked him why he drank the way he did.

"My father drank," came the pathetic reply. "He thought the answer to every problem was at the bottom of a bottle. I guess I just copied him. It's learned behaviour, and now I just don't seem able to stop."

"Do you have any brothers or sisters?" the social worker enquired, wondering if they also had followed the father's hapless example.

"Sure, my twin brother, Derek."

"Twin brother? Oh, I never knew that. Where is he?"

The prisoner told him where Derek and his family lived.

"May I pay him a visit?" asked the social worker.

"Of course. Why not?"

And so the social worker drove out to Derek's house. It was a beautiful, well kept home, and an attractive woman who turned out to be Derek's wife answered the door when he rang the bell. This did not look like the kind of place a drunk would live in.

Inside, the social worker discovered that Derek and his wife also had a couple of well mannered children. Explaining that he was there to try to find a way to help his brother to change his ways, the social worker eventually broached the delicate subject of alcohol. "May I ask: do you drink, Derek?"

Derek and his wife both laughed. "Heavens no!" Derek exclaimed. "I've never touched a drop in my life!"

The social worker was amazed. "Why not?"

"Well, my father thought the answer to every problem lay at the bottom of a bottle..."

Do you see? Twin brothers saw the same behaviour and grew up in the same environment and share the same gene pool and yet one sees the father's drunkenness as a reason to copy it and the other as a reason to avoid it at all costs.

You simply cannot hold your past responsible for your unwanted or unacceptable behaviours!

So what to do then?

First, don't go beating yourself up! The answer to shedding the past or present negative behaviours is not to replace it with another negative behaviour! There could hardly be anything more pointless than that!

So don't play the "blame game". That is: neither blame the past nor yourself. Instead, take *responsibility*.

## *Response-Ability*

I have already told the story of how, in October 2008 a previously reliable source of my income as a private psychiatric nurse became a trickle. In fact, it would be more accurate to call it an occasional drip. The phone was simply not ringing.

To get out of the situation and resolve the problem of there being not enough money coming in, something had to change.

What changed? A lucky break? A lottery win? Well, no. *I* changed, and all I changed was the question! I suddenly remembered that I didn't need to fall into the habitual, (and "normal"), pattern of asking repeatedly and uselessly "what shall we do?" It wasn't going to make the phone ring or change the economic climate!

With that realisation, I said to my wife, "We should ask a different question. We should ask how we are going to *be.*"

We decided to be *resourceful.* In other words, we made a decision to change our *state* regarding the situation before taking action *about* it. And what state had we been adopting? Well, worried, anxious, panicky … somewhere in that region. From that state of mind we were never going to solve the problem! Einstein observed that a problem cannot be solved in the same state of mind in which it was created, and if he says so, his authority is good enough for me!

It is worth noting about Einstein's thought that he is presupposing that the problem was created by you. It would have been easy to say in those circumstances that I didn't create the problem. It wasn't *my fault* that the world's economy was in such a shambles. (To be frank, listening to the news at that time, it was apparently *no one's* fault!)

But it *would* be true to say that I was creating the problem! The situation was simply the situation – a totally neutral thing. It wasn't malicious or personal; it didn't have the guns out just for me and my wife. Until I changed my question, I was simply viewing the situation as problematic.

And *that* is where the true solution lies. I changed my mind – an everyday procedure that we can all do at will with very little effort in most cases.

Note, please, that I'm not talking about merely changing my opinion. I changed my point of view, my perspective if you will.

A great doctor with whom I once had the privilege to work was a huge believer in supervision of clinical practice. His principle was that everything can be done differently – which may or may not amount to being done "better," he opined, but at least you would explore options that might never otherwise have been thought of.

Someone asked him one day why he thought supervision was so useful. He answered, as he so often did, by using a powerful and instantly understandable metaphor. He asked us to imagine that we were climbing a difficult rock face where we had to feel and reach for every hand and foothold.

He then asked us to imagine that someone, (he), was on the ground below with binoculars and some kind of microphone or megaphone. From his vantage point he would be able to see the next ledge easily. It would be a very easy thing for him to be able to instruct us, as the climber, to reach up and to the left or whatever it might be. From his place on the ground, compared to a climber, he did indeed have "super vision."

Regarding my flagging employment situation I could have played the "blame game." I could have said it was out of my control and there was nothing I could do about it and blamed the economic climate change for our dwindling finances. I might have garnered some sympathy from a few understanding friends, (most likely people who would also have wanted to bemoan their fate at the hands of the collapsing banks), but it wouldn't have paid any bills. That would have been pointless and useless.

Instead, I chose to change my *response* to the situation – an ability that all of us always have available. That is my *response-ability*.

I know you're itching to know if it made any difference doing that. The answer is emphatically *yes;* it made an immediate and very real difference. I had substantial income by the next morning!

That came about because as soon as I decided to be resourceful, *in that same instant* a new question popped into my head. I didn't have to struggle for it. There was no need to sit and ponder or scratch my head or furrow my brow. The new question was: What else could I do to generate income? In other words, what other *resource* did I have available to me or within me?

My next thought was, "writing." Again, this came spontaneously and without effort. That's important to note, and I realise I am writing a paradox here since I can't *tell* you not to make an effort because it will only make you make an effort not to make an effort!!

But that isn't intended to be an instruction. It is simply something you'll observe when you change your state of mind in this way. (Don't worry – I'm going to run through the process). You are equipped to solve problems, just as your body is equipped to heal wounds or fight infections. There is nothing you need to *do* to make those things happen. They are natural processes – nature gave them to you!

Now, this is my story of course. I happen to love writing, (you'd never have guessed, would you?), and in years gone by I have been paid for pieces I've submitted to magazines. That was nice, but a relatively slow process. The editors would sometimes hold onto pieces for months before telling you it had been accepted, and then there would be a further delay before the magazine itself hit the shelves. There could be yet another wait before the author's cheque was issued.

But this is the 21ˢᵗ Century. The internet exists and there are a zillion people with websites, blogs and other reasons to need written words. It didn't take me long to open an account with a freelance site, (www.elance.com), and put up my profile as a writer for hire.

I had a contract for a month's work and *a thousand dollars* by the next morning! (Curiously, although I have worked for a number of Elance's providers since then, I have never had a job offered so fast. There is just a sense of being "in the zone" and the doors just fly open for you in that state of mind).

A lucky break? Well, you may be able to claim that regarding the thousand dollar contract, but you most certainly can't say that it was luck coming up with the idea of writing for money. That was a direct and immediate result of changing my state – or, if you prefer, of changing my response to a situation.

I hope I have once and for all laid to rest any confusion about the difference between "blame" which is an awful, guilty feeling from which no one benefits, and "responsibility" which is an in-built natural mental resource available to all humans and simply means the ability to change your response to *anything*. What's more, the change is instantaneous and under your control!

## *How To Overcome Your Past By Changing Your Mind*

Remember, the sequence we have been taught habitually to follow, like traffic lights, goes like this:

## *DO* ➔ *HAVE* ➔ *BE*

As I pointed out earlier, this translates into things like *do* work hard through your education so that you can *have* a good job and then you will *be* happy. (Often it is the parent giving this advice who at least believes that he or she will be happy if you follow it).

Again, this isn't about blaming anyone. Not only would that miss the whole point, but it wouldn't be fair either. If you had parents who advised you in this kind of way, they almost certainly meant well and besides, they too had parents who would have imposed *their* beliefs and values on them! Indeed, you can take this logic right back to the Garden of Eden or the time of the dinosaurs if you wish. No one will be one jot better off for doing so! It is, quite simply, pointless at best, and damaging to otherwise perfectly good relationships between generations at worst.

If you have kids of your own, would you want them to think of you in this harsh way? And if they do, will it help them or you to a better future or better relationship?

It is your *response-ability* now, in this lifetime, in this very moment – now that you know there's another way – to make the change for yourself. You don't have to make a song and dance about it. You can do it quietly and subtly, but as you change you will discover that you've inadvertently raised the bar for others. You will become something of a role model, even a leader. This doesn't mean you have to go about telling people what to do, any more than many of the people who've influenced you throughout your life directly told you what to do. Just trust me on this – people will admire you from near and far. Just don't make that the *reason* for doing this. People admire oak trees too, but the acorns don't brag about what they did!

The alternative, by the way, is that your legacy will be that you're remembered as something of a warning. After you're gone, people will say of you, "Remember Joe Bloggs? He just would never change and he never fulfilled any of his dreams. He just didn't have the courage to try …" Whilst that just *might* be a way to influence those who come after you to change, it's not a guarantee, and besides, it's hardly any good to you right now while you're still here, is it?

The sequence you need to follow, you'll remember, is:

*BE* ➔ *DO* ➔ *HAVE*

Everything becomes simple and flowing when you do this. Choosing how to "be" means choosing a feeling state that feels good to you and everyone around you. Be loving, be kind, be creative, be fun … there are dozens to choose from, and endless variations on each one after that.

Just do a reality check here. What is your "default" state of being? If I were to conduct a poll of people who know you reasonably well, say your colleagues and half a dozen close or semi-close friends, and ask them to sum up your general character in a single word, what would most of them say?

Would they say

Serious?
Anxious?
Difficult?
Complicated?
Worrier?
Procrastinator?
Irritable?
Unpredictable?
Unreliable?

...or might they offer up such delights as:

Kind?
Thoughtful?
Generous?
Genuine?
Loyal?
Fun?
Reliable? (bit dull!)
Ingenious?
Helpful?

... or something related to those types of qualities?

If, by chance, you think the answer might be:

Clever
Fashionable
Obsequious, (means fawning a**e licker!)
Ambitious
Shallow
Full of him/herself
Dull
Geek
Show-off
Flirtatious

...or even worse, then you are leading with your ego! That isn't going to score you any Brownie points with anyone except other egomaniacs with whom you will mostly be in competition! Not only that, but it isn't going to win you a fulfilling life. Even if you have all the trappings of success right now – top salary, smart home and car, glamorous lovers even ... all of this will fade. (If you are in that bracket, I'm guessing you wouldn't be reading this if you didn't already have a strong sense that that is the case, so I'm not going to dwell here).

If you have trouble with this exercise try imagining what people might say standing at your graveside. It's a little maudlin perhaps, but worth it! If you have any suspicion at all that people are going to say you were egotistical, selfish, dull or any other quality you'd rather not be remembered for, you'll have discovered a powerful lever that will get you changing faster than Ebenezer Scrooge on Christmas morning!

There is no single definition of success, but for me I feel successful when I feel good about what I do all day while I'm doing it, go to bed at night feeling good about what I did and look forward to whatever I'm going to do tomorrow. That can be writing another chapter of this book, doing a day's nursing in a psychiatric ward or spending time with my wife – as long as I make her smile. Accoutrements are not necessary for any of this. (Okay, I have a computer on which to write my book, but it could be done with a pen and paper!)

Am I saying I don't like nice and/or expensive things? Not at all! I'm simply saying they will show up as a result of my *being* and *expressing* more of who I am and by making other people feel good by doing so.

My advice, then, is if you haven't already done so, is to pick a state from the second list, (or make up one of your own of course, but check that it fits that category). And if you want a category name for that list, I'd personally call it "spiritual" – but don't let that put you off. It really means expressing your true humanity, and has the same root as the words "inspired" and "in spirit." You may also like to note that "inspiration" also means "to breathe in" – and as long as you keep doing that, you're alive! Breathing out – or expiration – is the *last* thing you'll ever do, so you might want to be grateful for your in-breaths!

## *More About State Management*

Managing your state is going to change your life, so this isn't something you reserve only for emergencies. You should learn to do this as readily as you learned to operate the foot pedals in your car. It's for everything, all the time. Make it a habit.

Most of the time, most of us are going about are business being no more aware of our state of mind than we would be of our underwear.

There is one state of mind that is worth bringing to awareness and practicing like crazy. It is the state most people would wish to have in almost any situation and yet it is often overlooked as if it didn't matter.

I'm speaking of *peace of mind*. To have peace of mind no matter what comes your way surely would have to be the greatest blessing anyone could ever wish for, wouldn't it? I don't mean a stoical detachment or a cold-hearted lack of care. I mean the ability to deal with life's storms as well as its sunnier days without losing your cool or your faith in things turning out all right.

You will have to deal with life's messier and nastier bits. Everyone is going to experience a death or several – from your pet goldfish to your grandparents and maybe a few friends and closer relatives. The older you get, the more people will disappear from your life that way.

You're going to have to deal with a certain amount of physical pain and a quantity of emotional pain too. Any notion that life "should" be lived without such events is cloud cuckoo land as far as I can see, and anyone who thinks it could be done is certifiable! More to the point, (and less facetiously), it wouldn't help!

To live in such a clinical world would be akin to being anaesthetised your whole life. Furthermore, you'd have no friends because you'd have no understanding of their problems or plights would you?

Of course, all of this isn't leading up to me saying there's only one state of mind you should aim for. Then you'd be a real "one trick pony" and a pretty dull one at that. You should be versatile and adaptable – that's how life gets handled by those who seem to be able to cope with anything.

So, how do you do it?

Well, here's that bit of theory I told you about. Remember, there are three elements to any state – they're there all of the time. It's just a case of becoming aware of them.

The first element is, you will recall, your body language or physiology. Even a tiny shift in this can massively and *instantaneously* change the way you feel. Suppose you're at a lecture about something – let's imagine it's vitally important that you get the core meaning of the talk for some reason. But you're just not understanding it.

You start to feel confused, frustrated, even anxious – especially if there's an exam riding on it for example. Just try sitting up straight, unfolding your arms and uncrossing your legs if they were folded or crossed. The first step is to notice how you're feeling, (i.e. become *aware*) and then "make friends" with those feelings. Get interested in noticing how you *do* boredom, frustration or anxiety! What do you do with the speaker's voice? What do you tune out, and what do you let in?

After a few moments of playing this way you will already have changed your state from what it was. Now, just *pretend* you're enraptured by the speaker and whatever is being said.

Immediately you'll discover the information going in when it wasn't before. Yet all you did was to sit up in an attentive posture!

You want to feel cool and relaxed at an important interview? Think of the coolest character you've ever seen in a movie and pretend that you are them. (I don't mean do an impersonation or accents or anything! That's going to get you locked up, not a job!) I simply mean just hold your head the way they do, maybe use your eyebrows or some other tiny subtle movement they make as you remember them doing. Walk as they do. Just three or four paces will do it. You'll come over all cool!

The key – and I can't say this enough – is to consciously choose how you want to be. You always have that ability. Always did, always will. The very fact that you are even exercising that choice will put you streets ahead of ninety-nine percent of any rival who, I guarantee, will never read books like these. Against the one percent who do, you've only got to be a fraction of a percentage point ahead of them on one thing, and you're in.

Try the same tactic if you need to be confident on a date, or asking someone out you've fancied for ages. Courage is a state of mind, not a quality some are born with and others lack!

Follow through by examining your beliefs and your inner dialogue as I showed you in Chapter 7 – "The Magic Formula."

There is no "handicap" you can name that somebody hasn't overcome in ways that you – and even I – may think is impossible. Only yesterday I saw a documentary on TV in which a guy who's spent all his life living on the ocean goes hunting under water. He spent almost three minutes sixteen metres below the surface of the ocean with a spear gun *on a single breath.*

Apparently he can do this for up to five minutes. (Do *not* try that!)

Physiologically, that shouldn't be possible. Medically, that man should be dead. But he's very alive and fit too.

I have heard Anthony Robbins tell of a man who suffered a heart attack during one of Tony's events in Hawaii. He had no life signs by the time the ambulance came for him and it was some forty minutes before they arrived at the hospital. The man "flat-lined" the entire way and the doctor had long declared him dead. But Tony wouldn't give up, and being an incredibly influential man, managed to persuade the medical team to keep trying to revive this man. *They succeeded.*

(In case you don't know who Tony Robbins[1] is, just spend a few minutes looking him up – especially on Youtube. He is the rock star of personal development and a truly inspiring human being).

Dr. Bruce Lipton, a biologist, realised that the traditional information he was teaching his students about DNA simply wasn't matching up with the results he was witnessing in his experiments. He left his teaching post because he refused to teach what he knew to no longer be true. He realised that our DNA is *not* fixed – but in fact changes according to our own strongly held beliefs. His book, "The Biology of Belief" is a paradigm shifter that will once and for all remove from your life any possibility of you ever laying blame for any part of your behaviour or health issue at the door of your genetic make up again.

There are no limits to what you can be or what you can achieve. Personally, I believe that perhaps there is a kind of cosmic limit

---

[1] http://www.tonyrobbins.com

on what each of us may *want* to achieve. I, for example, have never wanted to catch fish, (I don't even like the taste of them), so I would have no desire to emulate the underwater hunter, awesome though he is.

Your nature will determine your limits because there will be some things you simply aren't drawn to. But of the things you are drawn to, you are more than equipped to achieve every one of them.

I'm going to close this section on belief by summarising a fictional short story[2] I once read. It told of a man who awoke one sunny day and began to discover that everything he wanted was handed to him on a plate. Even down to his football team winning all of their matches, his credit card never expiring, the woman he fancied from afar simply offering to have an uncommitted sexual affair with him ... and so on.

When he decides to try his hand at golf, he finds he can soon get a hole in one on any golf course he chooses to play.

Eventually it is revealed to him that he is in heaven which turns out to be a kind of way station between this world and death. Heaven is where you get to do all the things you never did in life.

Our hero soon realises that the place is pretty quiet, and is told that that is because everyone who isn't there is dead – a choice they make whenever they are ready, *but which everyone eventually makes.*

Life in Heaven, it turns out, is life with no challenges. And that is quite simply pointless. A challenge, however, is what far too

---

[2] From "A History Of The World In Nine And A Half Chapters" by Julian Barnes

many people think is an insurmountable problem and a reason for giving up on their dreams.

## *Recognising and Dealing With Resistance.*

Resistance is a very useful concept if you're messing about with electrical currents and circuitry, but not if you're trying to improve your life. Then it simply gets in the way.

Let's try a simple example. Suppose you and I are having a conversation that goes something like this:

**ME:** Did you know that you can have your life any way you want it?

**YOU:** Really? How does that work then?

[I proceed to explain how it works to you. You listen and nod attentively and with considerable interest. When I've finished, the conversation continues like this]:

**YOU:** Well, it sounds wonderful, but nothing like that has ever happened to me.

**ME:** Have you ever tried what I've suggested?

**YOU:** No, but I know people who have. All that positive thinking stuff doesn't really work.

**ME:** Interestingly enough, I know people for whom it does work consistently.

**YOU:** Oh, they're just the ones who got lucky aren't they? I mean, all of this can be put down to coincidence, can't it?

I could go on, but I'm sure you recognise this kind of thought process. As a matter of fact, *I* recognise it because it has been the kind of inner dialogue I've had with myself countless times. These days it rarely shows up and if it does I treat it like a well meaning friend who's had a little too much to drink! I know he's wrong and I gently but firmly send him home!

What's really going on here is that you and I have different beliefs. We've both tried to introduce "social proof" as an argument to back up our respective underlying beliefs – yours that this kind of thing doesn't really work, and mine that it does. That, and our own experiences, as if that demonstrated anything "empirical!"

When you boil it all down, each argument amounts to only this:

*"The world is the way I say it is."*

As a matter of fact that's probably about the only truth we can trust. To my way of thinking, if I say the world is a place where things turn out the way I want them to – or better – pretty much all of the time, and you say the world is a place which is down to luck and where s**t happens quite often, I prefer my world, thanks all the same!

Scientists, along with philosophers, metaphysicians, prophets and religious leaders, each in their own particular way, have been trying to deduce how the world is since time immemorial. You'd think that after all of this time we might have reached a consensus!

The fact that we haven't is what is of interest to us here. Because what it all comes down to is that your beliefs are a series of decisions and conclusions you've drawn over the course of your life so far depending on nothing more than how much certainty you feel about each one.

There are to this day people who believe that there is a God. On the other hand there are plenty who believe that there is no God. Then again, there are millions who believe there are many gods.

This book isn't focused on that particular topic, although we've touched on it of course, but I merely use it as an example of how certain people can feel that something is so. In that particular instance, some people are still killing other people for not believing the same things they do!

Resistance, then, is nothing more than a greater feeling of certainty that your view of something is the last word on a topic and all alternatives, other than those that more or less fit in with your existing "paradigm" or model of the world, are to be dismissed. True, a few might be given some scrutiny, but you will always look through the lens of what you believe to be so, and hence such scrutiny will always be somewhat biased.

Having to reassess your world view is acutely embarrassing not to mention extremely uncomfortable.

This, then, is the reason why installing a new belief appears so darned difficult. It wouldn't be, except that the old beliefs don't like being displaced, let alone *re*placed!

## *The Simplest Formula Ever For Replacing A Negative Belief.*

Here it is, then. It doesn't even matter if you don't know what your negative beliefs are! I've read dozens of books that contain techniques for unearthing these "subconscious" beliefs and I've spent hours in anguish trying to figure out what mine might be on any particular topic and still I didn't see results.

The outcome of that pattern is that it makes you feel worse, because then you add guilt and self reproach to compound the misery you were already feeling. After all, if I am responsible for my circumstances, (you will reason), and my circumstances are not to my satisfaction, then I am the key element that will bring about the change I desire.

Since that change is not showing up, (your thought train will continue), then some negative belief, or a whole viper's nest of them, must be lurking somewhere in my (frustratingly inaccessible) subconscious. All I need to do is to figure out what it/they is/are, uproot them and replace them with their polar opposites and keep repeating the new incantations until I actually believe them and then my life will change!

Phew!

No wonder people don't get that figured out.

Here's a simple, gentle alternative that will work every time.

When something isn't working out you know, by definition and by default, how you would like things to be. Let's use the example of being stuck in single mode when really you'd like to find a suitable mate to fall in love with, but he or she is just not showing up.

You just need to invest a few minutes, (might be five, might be fifty, might be five hours or even a few days), in *vividly imagining how it will look and feel when he or she is in your life.*

Now look. People tell me all the time that they can't visualise. The reason they think that is because when you try to do something that's so natural it's almost like breathing - it sort of slips away from you.

Think of a time when you were planning a trip. Maybe you were going to be the driver or maybe you were going somewhere by public transport – flying perhaps – but whatever it was it took some planning.

If you had been unable to imagine the destination, the arrival and, supposing there was some desirable event at the end of it such as a holiday or a wedding, you would have felt some anticipatory excitement too. If you've ever "looked forward" to anything, you've visualised it in some way and you've imagined good feelings.

You don't have to "see" images the way you would at the cinema! A few people seem able to do this – I can't. Some people barely use visual images at all. One of my clients found the pictures he made in his mind very dull. But when we experimented with adding a musical "soundtrack" he became very animated and loved any experience he chose to add that element to. It turned out he'd once been a DJ and he had a passion for music.

With this exercise just find your way into your imagination by bringing to mind an example or two of the kind of thing I've just mentioned. You can even think about what you're going to do tomorrow, even if it's all routine stuff.

Imagining is a human characteristic, so there's no doubt that you do it, but lots of people seem to have their own unique "style" of doing it, so don't beat yourself up before you've even begun by assuming that you're doing it "wrong." All you are actually doing is making a process that's so common you've forgotten to notice it, conscious.

Now let's deal with the second objection which is likely to be: "But how can I imagine the person of my dreams when I don't know what she/he looks like or behaves like?"

Well, you probably know what you don't want them to look like, and you certainly know how you wouldn't want someone to behave, so you do have a starting point.

But really, none of that matters. What counts is that you know how that person will make you *feel* when you do finally meet up.

You can imagine their outline, the way they embrace you, the glow of romantic encounters, the excitement of meeting them again ...

The pictures, sounds and maybe smells you can imagine are triggers for the *feelings*. If there's no emotion, this won't have much power.

Experiment and find your way in – until it feels good. Very good.

And now comes the magic.

Simply send love to that set of imaginings. Love it like you love a cherished memory. Keep doing it. Other scenarios may spontaneously "develop" – that's fine. Pile on the good feeling and then send love to the "memory" (even though it hasn't happened yet).

Repeat daily – in fact whenever you catch yourself in an idle moment, but more specifically, whenever you catch yourself thinking or feeling negatively about your situation.

Soon you won't be able to think or feel negatively about it – and the more you practise this, the more rapidly you will erase the negative beliefs – and you may never discover what they were! Who cares?

Try this technique on any area of your life where you want some improvement. If it's a better bank balance you're after, imagine feeling prosperous. (Don't try visualising large numbers on your bank statement – you won't drum up much emotion for that. Instead, enjoy *spending* the money – and giving some away too. You can bring a lot of joy with gifts, of course, and the pleasure of giving is a very powerful emotion, especially if it's to a person, group or cause you feel passionately about).

## *Stop Being "Realistic!"*

One of the greatest and most powerful pieces of wisdom I've ever come across – which I confess it took me years to accept – is that what you perceive as reality with your five senses is NOT how things actually are!

It's how they *were.*

The simplest analogy I can give you to explain this is to imagine you are making a movie. The script is written and edited, and then casting done until eventually filming begins. Scene by scene, take by take, the movie is built. Then it is, of course, edited and produced in all sorts of marvellous technical ways before finally the finished version is released.

(Or something like that. Forgive my ignorance if you're in the film industry. I'm not. It's a metaphor, okay?)

Now you go and watch the movie. The story you see and hear unfold before you on the screen is not in fact happening now. Those actors and extras are, *at this actual moment* somewhere else, aren't they?

Most television programmes are the same unless they are being broadcast live. The chat shows and the dramas are, for the most part, recorded. The hosts, guests and all the cast have long since been tucked up in bed by the time you get to watch it.

What you perceive as your "reality" is much the same. The "recording" and the "plot development" and the "script writing and editing" happened in your head and heart.

*Your thoughts and emotions determine what you get – but there's a time lag.*

So, as you begin consistently sending love, (good feelings), to the scenario(s) you want you are, in effect, *writing the next scenes of your life.* After a while, they'll start to appear!

If this sounds wild and wacky to you, don't worry. There is science that backs it up, although not all scientists agree about just how it works, or even how much it works. Most, however, do now agree that everything that appears solid in our universe is in fact comprised of packets of energy. Energy vibrates and certain frequencies harmonise with others of a similar nature, whilst others will cancel each other out or cause disharmony.

Think of music. Certain notes sound beautiful together, whilst others make you want to clap your hands over your ears until it stops.

You radiate energy. You instinctively know if you feel good around someone or if they make you want to run in the opposite direction whenever they're in the room. Your thoughts and feelings give off certain frequencies, (these are measurable), and those will harmonise with others – so the more you give off good and positive energy the more you will find good and positive things and people showing up in your life.

Still don't believe me? No matter. Just try it. The worst that can happen is that you'll feel good every day. How awful would that be?

## *Your Friends Mean Well But ...*

I'm sorry to have to break this to you, but a lot of people aren't too comfortable with happy people. In fact, some of them are downright miserable around happiness.

I know that sounds crazy. Why would anyone not want to be in the company of someone who is joyful and who makes other people feel good?

Well, of course, *everyone* would like that, but there are plenty of people who are, sadly, entrenched in their set of beliefs that it just doesn't ever seem to come their way. Good luck is for other people, they believe. They've tried love and got hurt, they looked after themselves and got sick, they started businesses and lost their shirt ...

We've all come across people with stories such as these.

You may be close to some of them. Maybe a parent or two has that type of outlook, or a sibling of yours ...? Possibly, you need only to look in the mirror ... but I wouldn't dare to suggest such a thing!

(It's a joke, okay?)

There are plenty of folk, however, who do believe that the world is a pretty miserable and hostile place and that to survive you need a good dose of luck. But it's mostly misery from the cradle to the grave.

> *"Most people tiptoe through life hoping to make it safely to death."*
>
> *– Earl Nightingale, co-founder of the Nightingale Conant corporation.*

Einstein is credited with having said that the most important decision anyone could ever make was that of deciding whether the universe was a friendly or a hostile place.

Now, I'm not burying my head in the sand. *Horrific* things happen. But embroiling yourself in them by watching and otherwise absorbing this drip-feed of misery on a daily basis won't solve anything. It'll just make you more miserable.

So stop watching the news. Seriously. You can't ever get miserable enough to make a difference to anyone else's misery. But you can *instantly* eliminate some negativity by making somebody laugh or feel loved or appreciated. Sometimes, the simple acknowledgement of a "thank you" can change a life, or at least make someone's day. And for all you knew, that person was thinking of suicide that day.

There is global misery – such as wars and famines and plagues – and there is personal misery, which is the insidious kind that's so much harder to get away from than the news because you can't switch off your friends, family or colleagues.

I'm thinking of the people who complain about their jobs or their aches and pains constantly. Or they're the ones moaning about their mate, or their lack of one. (Who wants to spend their life with a pain-in-the-butt anyway?)

This is a chorus. You hear it everywhere. People asking "How are you?" and getting the response, "Mustn't grumble," (meaning "I've got plenty to grumble about but it's not supposed to be socially acceptable).

How often do you hear anyone respond by saying, "I'm having a great life, thanks!" No one? Here's a tip for you. No, actually, let's make that an *instruction*. Be the first in your neighbourhood/workplace/family to do that!

You *are* having a great life when you think about it. It's the "when you think about it" that's the important clause in that sentence. Mostly people don't think about it. They get swept along by the general culture of moans and groans.

Therein lays your problem. It's the general culture. You have to stop being a part of that. That doesn't mean you should drop all of your friends – they sift themselves into those who want to be inspired by the new you and those that prefer to stay in the trench of misery in their own good time.

It means you need to become *aware* of your thoughts and feelings, and take responsibility for putting a positive spin on moans, gossip and other general low energy communications. They serve *no one.* You don't feel better for hearing it and the person who's doing the moaning doesn't either. They are simply looking for the next ear to bend about something they don't approve of.

Focus, just for a few moments, on your life. I don't know who you are or anything about you, but I know this much:

- No matter how little money you have, you have more choice available to you of what you will eat today than all the kings and queens of history did, *combined.*
- You can *read.* (Self evidently).
- You have had some kind of education.
- You almost certainly have a warm bed to sleep in tonight and a roof over your head.
- You are not starving or dying of thirst. (Millions are).
- You are not in agony, and if you are unfortunate enough to have a painful condition I can almost guarantee that that pain is managed.
- In general, you have access to outstanding health care.
- You have access to immense knowledge and information via the internet, (even if you don't own a computer, libraries do).

I'm sure I could think of more – but those are just a handful of *general* facts about the life you almost certainly lead as a citizen of a country where you can at least buy and read books.

If you add in the specifics about your life – your friends, who loves you, pets, privileges of all kinds, the sunset you saw yesterday, the vacations you've had, the laughter you've enjoyed, the freedom you have, the opportunities available to you … pause for breath …

… YOU HAVE AN *AMAZING* LIFE!!

And don't you forget it!

Sure, you can always find something to moan about! But what's the point? Change happens anyway. Stopping it is impossible, trying to is fruitless. Enjoy it, walk away from it, maybe even influence it – but don't try and *fight* it! If you are intending to be any kind of agent for change, and then decide what you are *for*, don't fight what you are against! That only fans the flames of it. Mother Teresa once famously declined to attend an anti-war rally, declaring that if they ever held a march *for* peace she would be the first one there!

If all of this moaning is so useless – indeed self-destructive – why is it so commonly indulged in?

The answer to that is very important, partly because it will help you to deal with those who do it, at least in your mind, and partly because it will help you to catch yourself and then stop yourself from doing it too.

*People complain about life because that's the only way left to them of feeling interesting.*

Read that again.

Vast numbers of people long ago gave up on their dreams, their hopes and their fantasies to face what they came to call "the facts" or "reality." They believe they are being "realistic" whereas in fact what they are doing, (as you now are beginning to understand), is living in the residue of all their past negativity, fears and doubts. Those in turn were probably passed on to them, however unwittingly and well-intentioned, by their parents who got it from *their* parents ... and so on.

That's why trends, including health and good or bad "luck," seem to run in families.

In case you are struggling with this piece of human psychology, let me give you an example that should make it clear. I've not only seen this one time and time again, but I have to confess that I was on both the receiving and giving ends of it at different times in my (earlier) life. I hope you – and those to whom I caused any distress – can forgive me!

Suppose you're a smoker and your best friend quits smoking. At first you would no doubt congratulate your friend, but after a while – as your friend seems to genuinely have walked away from his addiction – you find yourself uncomfortable with the situation.

You know it's the right thing to have done, but you start to convince yourself that you miss the camaraderie of smoking together. One evening, you and your friend are sharing a couple of drinks and you pull out your cigarettes. As you take one out to light it, you ask your friend, "Are you *sure* you wouldn't like one?" Your friend doesn't miss a beat.

"No thanks. I'm done with all that. But you go ahead."

Not a wince. You push a little harder. "Oh go on. Just one wouldn't hurt, surely? And we can sit on the wall outside and chat like we used to when we shared a smoking moment together. I miss those ..."

You can feel the guilt even as you say it. You know perfectly well that if your friend did take up the habit again you'd forever feel guilty. How would you feel if, in five or ten years, your friend was still smoking and got a diagnosis of cancer?

It's too awful to contemplate, but you can't now "un-say" what you've just said ... so you mentally beat yourself up whilst waiting to see on which side of the fence your friend will fall.

Okay ... let's end this horror story. Smokers do this kind of thing all the time to one another. It's not meant to be unkind, but they can never fathom the reason why they do it, so let me untangle it for you and then you'll see the broader picture too.

The person still smoking wants the friend to start again because she, (the smoker), is, of course, envious. Every smoker would love to quit, but most don't believe they'd make it.

And it's that belief – or rather lack of belief in themselves – that makes them try to get the friend to start again.

Imagine the smoker has fallen into quicksand. The friend has just freed himself from the quicksand. The smoker wants to get out too, but doesn't feel she can, so she'd rather have her friend back in with her.

That's a very crude analogy, but that is the mechanism that's going on.

And so it is with every relationship in all of society. Moaning is easier, (people believe), than changing. In fact, a huge number of people believe that "things" – not they – would have to change and since they don't really expect such "luck" they moan and groan about the way things are for them. And if they're not complaining they're worrying. I have yet to meet anyone who said that their problem was solved by worrying about it, or that they feel better for having indulged in a good worrying session!

Their friends, in order to stay friends, chime in, and if there are enough of them, an entire culture will develop where large groups will form to complain or worry about what they see as certain injustices or personal problems. No one feels good and no one grows. It is an endless loop tape of gloom and misery.

People want to be liked, and in order to ensure that, there will always be a pull towards the "lowest common denominator" which is often complaining.

The great self development teacher, Anthony Robbins has a marvellous story that illustrates this point beautifully.

As I recall it, he was asked to give an inspirational talk to the U.S. Marines – no mean challenge in itself! Of course, Robbins did a fantastic job, and afterwards he was allowed to play with some military "toys" – escorted by a very senior officer.

At some point during the VIP tour, the officer asked Robbins a question that made him stop in his tracks. The officer wanted Tony Robbins' view on why the young men and women of whom he felt so proud, never in civilian life seemed to achieve at the high level they did whilst serving in the Marines. The officer wondered if it was just excellent training, but having seen several generations of recruits come and go he felt there had to be something more.

Robbins agreed, and after a little thought he told his distinguished companion that he believed the root of the officer's observation was peer pressure. In the Marines, there was competitive spirit, a drive to excel and outdo each other. Whereas in civilian life, most environments default to the opposite. You aren't supposed to succeed more than your neighbours, family or friends. Many people are even conscious of a fear of outdoing their parents' successes.

No wonder, then, that so many people allow their dreams to fade and they themselves become mediocrities. It's easy to be accepted in life as a mediocrity.

But you didn't enter this life to be mediocre! (And neither did your neighbours, family or friends, for the most part). You wanted to have fun and joy and experience great adventures and do wonderful things! You wanted to inspire and discover and learn and grow. You wanted to feel passion in your heart and have a light in your eyes until the day you took your final breath!

What happened to all of that?

Here's what happened: you believed the lies!

- **Lie number 1.** Those who are in the majority must be right by reason of the fact that they're in the majority. Since the majority of people live mediocre lives and give up on their dreams that must be how life is "supposed" to be. You mistook "natural" for "commonplace." Back in the 1940s it was commonplace for people to smoke a lot, but it is natural to inhale poisonous fumes!

- **Lie number 2.** You thought there was no way forward. You got caught up in the lie so beautifully expressed by Earl Nightingale and quoted elsewhere in this book: "Most people tiptoe through life, hoping to make it safely to death."
- **Lie number 3.** Your parents knew best. No! Your parents almost certainly *did* their best – for you and themselves, given their culture and tools at their disposal, but only you know what is best for you!
- **Lie number 4.** Your head is more important than your heart. We live in a world that worships the intellect, facts and knowledge. We love logic and science. Can you tell me what is the science that makes a Beethoven symphony move you to tears?

  Your emotions are your guidance system. Your intelligence was meant to be it's slave – the computer that figures out what actions to take to bring about the results which the heart desires.

I'd like to offer what I consider to be the truth. You, or others are, of course, at liberty to disagree with me but before going down that road I would urge you to consider the following:

*I don't know if the following statements are actually "true" in the sense that they may or may not be provable by currently accepted scientific methods of testing. I only know that by adopting them **as if** they were true for me, my life has improved beyond all recognition in every realm.*

*I feel good all the time, I have great health and stamina, I have a wonderful loving marriage, great friends, work that I enjoy and money in the bank.. I live worry-free in a beautiful rural setting that makes my heart sing and brings me joy by doing nothing more than opening the curtains each morning and looking at the fabulous view.*

*My life is great, and it wasn't always so. Others who have followed principles similar to the ones I am about to outline appear to have had similar results.*

Here, then, are the antidotes to the lies above which I powerfully urge you to adopt:

- **Truth 1:** No one knows what is right for you except you. Following your "nature" is what is "natural" in your case, and every individual is different. If that were not so and we were all clones of one another, life would be bland and meaningless. It is differences and contrast that not only make life interesting but also supplies us with an endless array of wonders from which to pick and choose our personal "menu of life."

- **Truth 2:** There is *always* a way to move forward and to bring your dreams to life. That is the purpose of life. And the purpose of challenges and difficulties is merely to show you and bring into sharp relief what you *do* want. If there were no obstacles there would be no sense of achievement and no desire worth striving for anyway – hence, to all intents and purposes, no desires!

  To desire nothing would be a kind of comatose or zombie-like state where you would simply be waiting for death, (which would probably be much the same!)

- **Truth 3:** Your parents were struggling with the agenda set for them by *their* parents and culture. Your grandparents, in turn, were struggling with the agenda set by *their* parents and culture ... and so *ad infinitum*. Neither your parents nor anyone else can know what is best for you. If you are a parent, I would suggest that your job is to nurture and foster a belief in the heart's desires and let your children's spirits fly free – wherever they may be taken.

  None of this means that your parents were bad people, (though there may be a few, of course). But no one is ever given, or expected to take on, the role of controlling another regardless of the relationship that exists between them.

- **Truth 4:** Trust your heart's guidance at all times. It is your direct connection to the Divine Source from which you emanated and from which you have never been – and never could be – separated. Your emotions tell you what to do and what you want by letting you know what feels good and what doesn't. Your head's job is to figure out how to get from whatever "A" you're at to the "B" of your latest desire. It is NOT its job to have an internal battle going on and beat your heart's desires into submission!

Do those statements feel *good* to you as you read them? Is there a sense of relief somewhere that you can detect? Even if the feeling is, "If only life could be like that...!" you *know* there's something right about it.

That *is* how life is *"supposed"* to be.

And at this point, in all likelihood, you start playing the "blame game."

## *The Blame Game.*

The Blame Game goes something like this:

"Yes, it's all very well saying my life should be perfect, but you haven't been through what I've been through…"

And now out will pour a list of troubles, tribulations and a chequered past fraught with pain, dysfunctional families, losses, poor education, domestic violence, disease, political upheaval … you name it.

For every issue you can name, I can find you someone who's risen above it and led a fabulous life. I told you earlier the story of Oprah Winfrey.

How disadvantaged does someone have to be before you won't say, "It's all right for them … they had XYZ…"?

There *are* no excuses. There is *nothing* you can't rise above, change or overcome.

Your life, your history, your birth defects do not define you. Only you do that and that depends entirely on how you look at life, for which the shorthand is "attitude."

You get to choose your attitude. You get to choose what you focus on and how you direct your thoughts.

One choice is to blame anything or anyone you can think of. From God to the government to the colour of your skin – it's all the same.

The late, great motivational speaker, Jim Rohn used to say, "The same wind blows upon everybody. Whether you make it safely to where you want to go or not depends on the set of your sail."

To blame is to disempower yourself and also to *empower* the party you are blaming. Not only do you lose control of your own life but you allow someone or something else to dictate your level of happiness and your destiny.

Many people do this with their "significant other." They claim that he or she *makes* them unhappy. (We'll look at relationships in depth later).

Now this is where I get asked – no, *yelled* at – in my workshops, "So what's the alternative? You mean *I* should take the blame for everything that goes wrong in my life?"

No, I don't mean that. Blaming is a terrible, useless and painful thing to dish out, no matter who the recipient is. Worse, it makes no difference to the situation other than to sour relationships!

There is another alternative most people don't seem to have thought of: You can choose a different response to what's happening, (or what happened).

You have the *ability* to *respond* in any way you choose. We have a word, a very precise word for that talent too. It's "responsibility". Which is really *"response-ability."*

The word has become interchangeable with "blame" but they're not the same at all. Blame hurts, responsibility is freeing.

> **Golden Principle: You can *always* choose a different response.**

Have you ever found something funny that someone else just couldn't see the humour in? Or even found yourself laughing at some embarrassment that happened some time ago but now you can see the funny side of?

What's happened there? The event hasn't changed, but your perception of it, and hence your response has.

The key to doing that at will is in realising that you can, quite literally, see things from a different angle or perspective. Once you've practiced this even just a handful of times you will quickly realise that you are not at the mercy of your mood or mind, but you are in fact the master of it.

Knowing *that* makes you master of your destiny, and indeed able to take command of any situation.

## Just try this ...

Just for experiment's sake start with something mild. Think of a moment when you felt slightly uncomfortable in some way. Just take a few seconds to bring something to mind – something that makes you cringe or at least grimace a little when you think of it, but isn't life-altering.

Okay, got something?

Now, *notice how you notice it.* In other words, let yourself discover whether you *re-view* that incident by seeing pictures or hearing sounds primarily. (It's unlikely you'll remember in smell or taste as a primary sense but you could be the odd one out, so allow that possibility too).

I'm going to assume you see pictures in your mind just to demonstrate the principle. You'll soon get the hang of this.

Are your pictures moving, (like a movie), or still, (like a photograph)? Are they in colour or black and white? Do you see them as 2-dimensional, (as you would on a screen), or in 3-D such that you could move around them?

Do you see the image(s) through your own eyes, as if you were there again, or do you see yourself in the picture too?

Does the image appear to be framed in some way – i.e. it has edges – or is it panoramic, as in the way you would usually see things with your eyes?

Is there sound? Is it muffled or distinct? Loud or soft? Harsh or easy on the ear? Is it "surround sound" or does it seem to come from a single source?

You're getting the idea now, aren't you?

Take a few minutes to discover all of the qualities about how you perceive a memory that makes you uncomfortable. *You are discovering how you process information – and this discovery will give you immense power.* You will begin to experience the incredible truth that your brain/mind does not "run the show." You are *not* at the mercy of your moods, feelings or beliefs. You do *not* have to ever again say, "I can't help it – it's just the way I am," about *anything.*

Are you starting to see how you can take *"response-ability"* for your life?

Great!

Now, let's do some magic!

Play with those pictures! Allow yourself to discover what happens to the way you feel when you:

- Move the images further away
- Fade the colour to black and white
- Introduce some soothing music into the background.
- Let Bugs Bunny run across the "screen."
- Float above the image and get a bird's eye view of the scene.
- Turn the scenario into a Disney cartoon.
- Have a character slip on a banana skin. (Unless that was what happened to cause you embarrassment in the first place!)
- Try any other variation you fancy! (Have your favourite film star walk in, hear your lover whisper naughty things to you during the "action," see the whole thing running backwards fast, as if you were rewinding a video recording … )

Spend five or ten minutes playing in this way. When you've finished, notice what happens when you try to recall the original scene.

Even if you can remember the original event "as it happened" (and you probably can), the most important aspect to pay attention to is *how you feel*.

I guarantee you won't be able to bring the discomfort back. If you can, go back and play some more – until your tinkering at least makes you giggle.

Now did that take years of psychotherapy? Was there a requirement that you reveal all the skeletons in your cupboard to a paid nosey parker?

No!

You made yourself feel better about something without telling a soul what happened or how you brought the change about! Not only that, but it was easy and fun – and took just a few minutes.

Using techniques such as these, (and there are others), you can fix phobias in minutes, overcome shyness, anxiety or other life inhibiting habits – even addictions – in a single day.

You're in charge of it all. How you feel as well as what happens to you. Who you become, what you achieve and how much you love your life. Your whole destiny is within your control.

How excited are you about *that?*

So let's get on with it…

# 15: Empowering Relationships

"No one is an island" goes the old adage and yet we are living in a society that celebrates independence. The more you can do by yourself and for yourself, the more you will be encouraged not only to continue but to reach ever greater heights.

Until you fall – either from grace or off your pedestal.

Nobody and nothing can keep going in an upward direction indefinitely. (Fortunately, the corollary is true too, so you won't keep falling forever either!)

However, you simply cannot get very far by yourself, no matter how much you would like to foster the illusion. If you were left strictly alone you would wake up tomorrow morning with no running water to brush your teeth or make a drink with, no energy supply to your home, no way to refuel your car and no one to collect your household refuse.

That would be just the beginning!

Life without *interdependence* would be a nightmare. Survival and trade, amongst many other things that we take for granted as a part of every day existence, depend upon it.

The same is going to be true for you at a personal level. You would not – could not – have any sense of identity or individuality if you were the only person here! Think about that for a moment.

Your identity is *defined* by contrasting and comparing yourself with others. The problems that arise in relationships come partly from not realising that this is the case and partly from confusing contrast and comparison with *competition*.

There's an irony here. Growing up we want to copy our friends. Indeed, any parent of a child aged between about five to nine years old will tell you that all hell can break loose if your child thinks for a single moment that he or she will be the only one in class without the latest fad or gadget to show off to all their friends.

And then puberty strikes. As teenagers although we covet gadgets and fads, it becomes paramount to express our *individuality* as if being new and original was the very force of survival itself! Perhaps it is in a peculiar kind of way.

Odd fashions and weird food mixtures are the very currency of life. (I will never forget the teenage boy who proudly told me that his favourite snack was *vinegar* sandwiches. I never discovered how he kept the liquid filling inside the bread).

Of course, before long we want to explore the "forbidden" territory of sex and relationships. And for the first time we have to face the truth of whether or not we've done a half decent job on ourselves, because now the people we want to be most intimate with will give us disarmingly honest feedback. Are we or are we not qualified to be accepted and loved by those whom we most passionately desire?

For some it works relatively smoothly. For most, however, this is a painful but necessary rite of passage. Our rough edges are mirrored back to us by those who will force us to look at ourselves – a job our mothers and other well-meaning but spurned counsellors could never have done so effectively, if at all.

And so our journey of relationships begins. At this point we should pause and consider what relationships – the intimate kind – are actually *for*. Many people seem to feel that relationships are the opposite of loneliness; a kind of insurance policy against the dreaded "lonely old age."

The first point to make is that loneliness is a state of mind, whilst old age is merely a birthday count! I have been lonely in relationships, and have also met others who felt similarly. By contrast, I have been extremely happy in my own company during my single years. What we are dealing with here, as ever, is emotions – the foundation stone of states of mind which, in turn, are the building blocks of the behaviour that then shapes our destiny.

Having touched now more than once on the subject of emotions, it is time we explored the greatest emotional maze of them all: *love*.

## *Love*.

By touching on this subject we will uncover the greatest self help secret of them all. I will reveal it to you now because it doesn't need to be a surprise. Indeed, it should be blindingly obvious to us all, but it isn't for many, and I included myself in that large group for many years.

That last paragraph is a kind of caveat; a warning that once I show you this secret it may seem a little confusing. The words will have a ring of truth and yet at the same time you may well puzzle over how it is possible to live by this tenet.

Enough preamble. Here is the secret:

> **Golden Key Principle: You cannot receive what you will not give or do not have.**

We all want to be loved. The internet is peppered with dating sites where jilted and lonely men and women hang out hoping that someone will find them and fall in love with them. Their reasoning, (in the majority of cases), is that if the "right" man or woman should happen along and demonstrate that they unconditionally love the advertiser, then – and only then – might the advertiser reciprocate. Only the advertiser knows the "rules" of such behaviour, and even *they* are not conscious of what they actually are!

Phew!

In plainer English it goes like this: "I've been hurt by love before and you might hurt me too, but I'm willing to take a very limited risk with you. If, and only if, you can consistently show me unconditional love no matter how I show up, (i.e. damaged emotionally, even distant and uncommitted), then I might, in time, trust and love you back. But don't ask me for any guarantees or commitment until I'm good and ready. And no, I can't tell you when that will be. If ever."

It's not much of a deal is it?

And it's rendered even less likely to work because the unsuspecting respondent is likely to have a similar agenda.

You cannot "make love" – and you can take that phrase to mean anything you like – if you don't have the ingredients to make it with!

Consider a tangible example to make it easy to see why this is a recipe for either a guaranteed disaster or a relationship that won't ever get off the ground.

Suppose you are watching a documentary about poverty in the third world. You are deeply moved by it and decide you want to do something about it. You want, let us say, to build hospitals and schools. You may feel passionately about this.

There's just one problem. You're broke. Now you will just be left with frustration!

(Yes, I know you could raise money, but then you'd have money. Whatever way you look at it, this problem needs money to solve it).

You cannot solve a poverty problem by being poor yourself. You need the resource that will fill the need. Similarly you cannot love someone if you do not have a "bank account" with some "love credit" in it!

Whilst we're at it, let's take a moment to look at that from the recipient's end of things. Suppose you are an inhabitant of that third world country. Word may reach you that someone in the West wishes they could help but they have no money. You're grateful for the sentiment, but with a shrug and a sigh you realise that life in your third world country isn't going to change. Not today. Another day will go by without schools or hospitals.

By contrast, here comes some philanthropist with the funds to help you and your country. Would you not jump for joy?

Would that person not become a beloved hero in your life – and perhaps in the minds of many generations yet to come?

By giving you will receive. You will, in this example, receive gratitude and accolades and perhaps some honours. Who knows what the knock-on effects would be?

The principle here is simple. *Be a giver first.*

In order to do that you have to have something to give and you must be comfortable about giving it. A billionaire miser is not going to help that country, whereas a "poorer" philanthropist is.

Now, in case you're thinking, "It's all very well for the philanthropist – he's got plenty to begin with" I refer you to the story of the widow's mite in the Bible. This is not a tale encouraging you to live in poverty, but to give from your heart.

In order to be a giver you need to be selfish. Yes, you read that right; I said *selfish.*

## Be Selfish!

I'm not telling you to be mean or to hurt other people's feelings. "Selfishness" is another word we've misunderstood. (Blame being confused with responsibility was the last one, remember?)

When you're mean to someone you want everything for yourself, you want your own way and you're not about to budge an inch. That's nasty, but that isn't what I'm talking about.

I was once on a personal development seminar where someone in the group called the group leader "self-centred." He replied without missing a beat, "Well, where else is there for me to be centred?"

Nourish yourself if you want to feed the hungry. Enrich yourself if you want to help the poor. And love yourself if you want to give love!

There is a great truth in what I've just told you. The two-way street you want, need and expect from life *all exists in you*. If you want people to give back to you they won't if they perceive that you are already empty. Why? Because they will sense that *they* will get nothing back from you!

This is why we say "the rich get richer and the poor get poorer." It's not because rich people are greedy or mean. It's because others can see that they're worth investing in. This is true regardless of what form your riches take. Be rich in love and kindness, time and respect, as well as with things and money and you will prosper and flourish. You will be nurtured, loved and cherished.

Look after *you* first. You always need to have something to give. You can then afford to be generous with your smiles, your praise, your time, your energy, your things, your money and your love.

Just imagine how much you'll receive in friendship, laughter, gifts, opportunities and reciprocated love when you can live like that!

## *What Relationships Really, Really Are...*

In case you're thinking that relationships are just about how you get on with other people let me put you right on that score.

Relationships *define you.*

You couldn't know who you are if you had no basis for comparison or contrast. Think about it for a second: it's not hard to see.

If you had somehow been born and abandoned on a desert island, (and miraculously survived of course), you would have no way of knowing who or what you are. You would, presumably have some awareness that you existed, and your body would give you signals that would get your attention, like hunger for instance.

The premise of Rudyard Kipling's "The Jungle Book" is that Mowgli, abandoned as a baby and brought up by wolves, thought he was a wolf at the outset of the story. Jodie Foster stars in a film called "Nell" (a wonderful piece of acting), where she plays a woman who has lived entirely alone and "wild" for most of her life.

And Neale Donald Walsch, in his wonderful "Conversations With God" series of books, asks us to consider waking up and floating in a completely white environment with no features of any kind. In other words, you would be weightless and "experience-less." We are then asked to imagine a tiny black ink dot on one white wall. Then, and only then, do you get a sense of "self *and* other."

You cannot know you – or even *be* you – without others to relate to.

Now, consider this scenario. Your best friend calls you up in a state of great excitement and tells you that he has met the partner of his dreams. You simply *have* to meet her. He's arranged a gathering of several close friends in some bar tomorrow night and there is no way you are saying no to this invitation. He's most insistent!

So you go to the rendezvous fully expecting to be blown away by your buddy's new girlfriend.

You meet ... and she's a horrible disappointment. To *you*. Your friend is clearly besotted. When the evening's over, you inevitably will compare notes with the other friends who were there. Is everyone going to feel as you do about this woman?

Probably not. Opinions and perceptions will vary. It's also highly unlikely that anyone else is going to feel as your friend does either. After all, he's fallen in love with this person, (Of course, it's possible that someone might, and in that case you have the beginnings of a soap opera script!)

The point is this: it isn't just beauty which is in the eye of the beholder. It's *everything*.

No one is objectively, empirically loveable, any more than anyone is measurably, definitively despicable. It's *all* a matter of opinion – of subjective judgement.

Hmmm. That's something to think about isn't it? Because if you extrapolate from that what you'll soon see is that *the attributes you see in others can only be projections from yourself.*

People mirror back to you what you see, or don't want to see, (but others can), in yourself. Think of it like being told you snore. You aren't aware of it and probably would never know you were doing it if it weren't for someone pretty close to you, (in every sense of the word), telling you that you do!

The same is true of difficult or unpleasant characteristics. If you find someone boring, (and especially if that person keeps showing up in your life), then yes, you have a boring side to you too. The mirror doesn't lie!

Indeed, whenever you find yourself criticising, berating or gossiping negatively about another person, group, organisation, nation or government, what you are picking out is, in some way, what could also be picked out about you!

Uncomfortable, isn't it?

Yes, but it's extremely useful and empowering.

Perhaps you can see the truth now in the old adage that judging someone else does not define them; it merely defines *you* as someone who needs to judge!

Just think for a moment about how come you can identify those particular characteristics. Think back to the "best friend's girlfriend" scenario. Let's suppose you thought she was "boring" but another friend found her "deep and interesting" whilst a third thought she was "charming." If we were to ask the poor woman to describe her own personality it's hard to imagine that she would describe herself as "boring" isn't it? (Fortunately, she's entirely fictitious, as is the situation, so don't fret about her).

Any characteristic you can perceive is only possible because you have a reference for it in your own "internal library." It's like the black dot on the white wall. Now you have experience of black dots and you'll know another one if you encounter it.

This is clearer sometimes if you consider physical characteristics. If you look in a mirror you start making judgements (usually negative!) about yourself. "I'm starting to look old" or "I need to lose some weight" are common bits of self talk. But how do you know?

Only because you have compared yourself with other people who are younger or slimmer than you. Not only that, but you have then made some generalised assumptions about how younger or thinner people are perceived compared to how you imagine they will perceive you. You are also assuming that when others look at you they will see – and judge – everything the same way you do. Plastic surgeons make a very good living out of this flawed thought process!

Relationships, then, are reflections of you. If you have a pernicious boss it might be worth your while considering that he or she isn't universally despised. Some people will like that person, not least the people who appointed them to the position of power. Their perniciousness is impinging on you so that you can heal it in yourself!

In other words, if you're conscious of it, you can act on it.

How you do that is simple enough. You can adapt the memory-changing technique I showed you in Chapter 10, (in the "Blame Game" section).

Wait until you're alone and calm! (Don't try this when you're angry – you just won't get there).

Bring the person you're struggling with to mind and as before start experimenting with the "movie" in your head. Shrink the image to the size of a pinhead, drain the pictures of colour, turn the person into a cartoon character … just *play*.

Keep doing it until bringing the person to mind doesn't bring up anger or whatever negative emotion you were having. This is a great technique to use on ex partners where there is some acrimony by the way!

To put the icing on the cake, you can create what I call a "future memory." (Yes, I know it's an oxymoron). What I mean by that is you play out a scenario in your mind that has not yet happened but which could and which involves this other person. It needs to be something that *would have* brought the difficult emotions to the surface, only now the way you play it out, it all works out well and you both feel good about whatever transpires between you.

Try it. It's amazingly powerful as well as comforting. Not only that, but it's astonishing how often things change between the parties concerned.

I don't know for sure how this works, but since I believe that everything is energy and is also interconnected, it isn't too much of a leap to suppose that this kind of concentrated focus alters the dynamics of the energy exchange between the two of you.

It doesn't matter how it works. It makes you feel better. It changes at least two lives for the better more often than not. (If you find no effect the first time you try this, do it some more!)

Whatever you do, don't dismiss this powerful technique as something that probably won't work because it's all imagination. Leaving it here on the printed page is pointless and you have absolutely nothing to lose by giving it a whirl.

Once again, you don't need years of psychotherapy to bring about desirable, positive change.

In the next chapter, we'll turn our attention to the almost equally important subject of wealth and money. When you're ready …

# 16: Wealth

Money is …

How would you finish that sentence?

Is it the "root of all evil?" Or the solution to all your problems? The question is not, "Which of those is true?" but "Which *feels* truer for you?" How much money you have as well as how much you get to keep and enjoy will depend to some extent, though not entirely as we shall see, on how you *feel* about the topic.

Of course, you could have come up with the pragmatic response: Money is a means of exchange. That would also be true, but until you get clear about your relationship with money there may be severe limitations on what you can exchange it for due to a general lack of it in your life.

Money is something you need to have a defined relationship with, much as you would with a member of your family, a friend or even a pet. In fact, thinking of money as a pet will serve us well as an analogy because the pecking order in this relationship should most definitely be that you are the master whilst it is the servant.

Far too many people have it the other way around.

I'm going to propose that we end the sentence this way:

*"Money is … a measure of appreciation."*

There! That didn't hurt did it? It's just a kind of applause, an expression of gratitude for a service rendered or goods received.

Since this is a book on self help, you may even have wondered why there is a chapter on money at all. Isn't money something you simply earn as a result of hard work?

That is a commonly held notion, and it is a very popular one with politicians who like to keep the population believing that. They get a lot of taxes that way as well as a work force of whom many will do the most undesirable tasks in the belief that they have very little, if any, choice.

There is *some* truth in it, but it's equivalent to saying that the North Pole is a place you can get to if you walk far enough. It's true, but no one really wants to do it that way in the course of normal daily life.

The bottom line is this: millionaires and billionaires have exactly the same number of working hours available to them as those who are struggling on the bread line. Furthermore, there are plenty of extremely wealthy people who have poor educational backgrounds and/or a bad start in life in some other way. Financial success cannot, when you analyse the evidence, be attributed to a single external factor – or even a combination of them. If it was possible to say that all people of a particular ethnic origin, gender, gene pool, educational status or anything else stood more chance of becoming financially wealthy than other members of the human race, I feel very certain that someone would have worked that out by now.

It's all a matter of luck then, is it?

To my way of thinking, this is the last excuse available for anyone who doesn't make it to financial freedom, but it is no more than that I'm afraid. It's an excuse and a lie.

The answer has the same root principle as I gave you in the chapter on love and relationships. It all depends on how much you are willing to give – in terms of passion, time, energy and dedication.

Sounds like another way of saying "hard work"? You're wrong! This is the complete opposite!

I'm talking about loving whatever you do, freewheeling through life, without the need to be shackled by a "job" or a contract.

To achieve the life style I'm suggesting requires belief in yourself and trust in something greater than you – whatever you choose to call that. It requires that you follow your heart and give from it, whatever that means to you. You must *add value*.

Let me give you an example which I'm sure will make this clear. I'll begin by asking you a question.

Who are the highest paid people in the world? In general terms, I mean. Doctors, perhaps? (Not even close!)

Teachers? Certainly they deserve to be high on the list but we all know that isn't the case.

Surely not politicians? Well, many do better than teachers, nurses and a lot of doctors, but no, it isn't them.

The highest paid group of people in the world are *entertainers.*

Heck, they can even go on earning millions after they're dead! Our singers, actors, sports personalities, chat show hosts and disc jockeys – the ones at the top of their game anyway – earn millions upon millions year after year. Why?

*Because they make us feel good.*

This isn't a grudge, by the way. I think they're worth every penny. I've paid the equivalent of a slap-up meal for about six people to get one ticket to a decent concert by an artiste I love. I've done that more than once, and I'd do it again. I've travelled long distances to be at events too.

Does this mean you have to be an entertainer to be rich?

No, of course not. But you can't get rich by trying to be Ebenezer Scrooge either – trying to get as much as possible while giving as little as possible. (Scrooge was lucky – he had a family who remembered when he was still a nice guy and who forgave him, and so were willing to accept him as he was even before the three ghosts gave him the backside-kicking of a lifetime!)

You can't just give any old thing. You can't use trickery to make money. If our top singers decided to switch to playing football, whilst the footballers decided to start making music albums, they'd all lose their audiences pretty darned quick. (Unless they were doing some kind of charity gig of course, in which case they'd garner even more love).

That's the key though – when you do what you love – and yes, you do need to do it well – people love the love in you.

You'll get paid – a lot – for being yourself, whatever your field of endeavour, as long as when you're being you, you're giving out a lot of love.

Now, the sharper-eyed among you may have noticed that we've switched subtly from talking about what you can *do* to make money to how you can *be* that will simply attract money.

> ***Golden key principle: BE first, then DO, then you'll HAVE all you want!***

Consider my definition of money I made earlier: *Money is a measure of appreciation.*

Turn that over in your mind for a moment or two. Can you think of a time when you happily paid money for something that you didn't appreciate? Think of all the restaurants you've eaten in, the theatres and cinemas you've sat in, the bus or taxi rides you've taken, the food you've bought in supermarkets …

Now add into the mix the bills you pay. Aha! You probably don't like those do you? But just think for a moment. Your energy supplier gives you a vital, life supporting service *on credit*. It doesn't ask you what your earnings are or indeed anything about your personal circumstances. It's taken as a given that you need heat, light and clean water to live.

Then there's your mortgage. When I bought my first home, the mortgage broker I saw was a droll Yorkshire man. I told him I wanted a mortgage and he said dryly, "No you don't. No one wants a mortgage. What you want is a *home*."

He was right of course, but at the time buying a home for cash wasn't an option. Someone was willing to let me live in a dwelling of my choice, and which I could call my own *even though I didn't have enough money to buy it.*

As for taxes, the bane of everyone's financial existence it would appear, society as we know it would simply collapse if there were no taxation. Do you want cared for roads to drive upon and your streets lit at night? How about help with health care, pensions and some kind of welfare?

Now, of course I've strayed into politics. (I've touched on religion already! How brave am I?) It may be true that you don't get anything for nothing, but neither will you get nothing for what you give!

You and I live in the most abundant times in all of history. Even the poorest of us can wander down to a supermarket and choose the ingredients for today's dinner from a cornucopia so vast that all the kings and queens of history would have gasped at what's available. Growing up in England as I did, I remember my father telling me how much he enjoyed avocado pears when he had taken a trip to Africa in his youth. I could only imagine avocados. But now they are as available to me as English apples in any high street.

I'm making an attempt here to get you to look at money – including the money you pay out – differently. Don't begrudge it; it's paying for the society that has given you, me and our children and grandchildren more than any generation in all of history.

Yes, I know and I would agree that our society has much to be done to it before we might declare it perfect, but I also know that pointing out its flaws and moaning about it only adds to the problems, as well as making you feel bad, and that is utterly pointless and futile.

If you want to improve society, be a role model of joy, optimism and positivism. Spread happiness, don't add to misery!

Money ebbs and flows in your life like breathing. Try breathing in ... and holding onto it. You need to breathe in to live, but if you don't let it go you won't last long. In fact, you can't even do it! You *have to let go.*

Breathing out enables you to breathe in again so that you can carry on living.

Paying out enables you to remain grateful and appreciative of what your money has bought so that you have the energy and the freedom to express yourself – whatever it is you do that makes other people feel good – so that more money can come back into your life.

It's called "currency" because it's a current, like water or electricity. It has to flow or it can't function. Try accumulating money and spending none – you'd soon end up on the streets. Indeed, there have been a few eccentric folk who've done just that: died sleeping rough in rags only to have the posthumous discovery made that they were millionaires.

## Why Do You Want To Be Wealthy?

I might have done better with some readers if I'd asked simply, "Do you want to be wealthy?" since a lot of people say they actually don't want a lot of money.

When people say this, a little digging almost always reveals that they hold a belief such as, "Money doesn't bring happiness," or "I wouldn't know what to do with it."

The first is an acknowledgement of fear – which is a kind of fear of the unknown for anyone who's never experienced wealth. The second is an admission of defeat when it comes to fulfilled dreams.

There is, in fact, only one thing to do with money ultimately, which is to spend it. Of course you can save it so that you can spend it later on large things or projects, or you can give it away so that someone else can spend it, or you can leave it in your will, in which case, once again, someone else will spend it, in most cases your children, but sometimes it's the cats' home. If you have a lot more money than you need for your personal requirements, (when you would be classified as wealthy), you are in a position to help others who are in some need. So to say you wouldn't know what to do with it is very short-sighted. You'd have no shortage of people offering their ideas of how you might spend it I can assure you!

As for the belief, money does indeed not bring happiness; neither does it bring misery. Money is in fact perfectly neutral in the matter of how you feel. Only you can decide whether to be happy or not. It isn't dependent on your bank balance!

It is, however, worth pointing out that severe lack of money is almost always accompanied, in general, by crime, disease and many premature deaths from both. Whilst there are people living in abject poverty who are very happy, that doesn't mean that some creature comforts wouldn't go amiss. There are still far too many areas of our world that have yet to acquire things that you and I pretty much take for granted, such as hospitals, schools, hot meals and clean water.

There may be other negative beliefs or excuses you use to convince yourself that life lived from payday to payday is all right, but I've never yet heard anyone say they didn't really want their pay rise or bonus when they've eventually shown up.

The great personal development teacher Anthony Robbins said, "Money won't solve all your problems. But it will allow you to arrive at them in style."

For our purposes, in this author/reader relationship that we have right now, I'm going to assume that you wouldn't be reading a book such as this one if you didn't at least want *some* more money.

I mean, how would it be if you could increase your annual income by, let's say twenty five percent this year? How about fifty? Dare to dream here ... how about *doubling* your income?

Wow! Think of that. Twice your income in the next twelve months. Is a dream holiday hoving into view? A new car, a longed for new wardrobe, perhaps?

You could add an extension to your house maybe, or even pay the mortgage off in half the time – if not altogether.

Aha! Now you're getting the idea! And just as you're starting to enjoy that experience of dreaming those daydreams, allow yourself to discover what happens if you add a couple of noughts onto that doubled figure? How about *three* zeros?

Let's just make up some numbers so you can get an idea of what they look like. I do realise this is a silly game inasmuch as I have no idea what you earn to begin with, and even if I did, in five, ten or twenty years time, these numbers will look ridiculous. Should my book still be read a century from now, no doubt readers will laugh at the kind of pittances I'm about to suggest, but given that everything is relative, you can insert your own numbers and even switch to your own currency if you like.

I'm British and we still have pounds and pence, so I'm going to give my example in that currency, okay?

Let's suppose you currently earn £25,000 a year. That, in 2011, isn't too bad. There are a lot of people on about half that salary right now. This is the kind of money a nurse can earn, maybe a senior manager in a retail business, or a middle of the range chef in a nice but not too expensive restaurant or hotel, for example.

So let's double it.

Now you're on £50,000 a year!

Looks nice, doesn't it?

Just spend a few moments getting your head around what double your salary would mean in real terms. How much would you bring home after deductions each pay day? How nice would that feel to have all that money left over?

Okay, now let's add two noughts ...

£5,000,000

That's five *million* pounds a year! We're not talking about a windfall, this is an average annual take home pay for you. You're in serious Rolls Royce territory now. Try to imagine your life style with *twenty times* your present salary.

And now let's add that extra zero. Ready?

£50,000,000 a year!

*Fifty million pounds personal income per year.*

This is a vast sum of money. This is the kind of money that would enable you to run your own empire. You could own airlines, islands, news media ... in fact, you probably would own some or all of those things to generate that kind of money.

Let's just add a little reality and context to our dreaming here. Within the last three years, Bill Gates, the founder of Microsoft, (from which he resigned as an employee in 2008), is estimated to have earnings that look like this:

$250 per second
$20 million a day
$7,300,000,000 a year

In British pounds, that's going to approximate to £5,000,000,000 a year! (That's five billion pounds in case you don't know what to do with nine zeroes!)

Bill Gates dresses in ordinary clothes, (okay, nice ones, but he isn't dripping with gold). Bill and his wife Melinda have a foundation which is helping to both save and improve the world.

I've never heard him say that he doesn't know what to do with the money.

It is my observation that private individuals like Bill Gates, Richard Branson, Anthony Robbins, Elton John and countless others who are personally wealthy do far, far more to make this world a better place than any government has done or will ever do in all of human history.

Are you getting more comfortable with the prospect of being wealthy now?

Good! Then let's get to it!

## *Where The Money Is...*

If you want more money, where do you go? The bank, maybe? Or perhaps you ask your boss for a raise or you look for a better paid job. Or you sell something.

You may or may not succeed in generating a little cash influx in some or all of these ways, but there is a bottomless well of money available to you if only you would do two things. First, you'd have to be willing to look into this well. And secondly, and perhaps far more important, you need to believe that the money really is where I say it is. If you don't, you won't look into the well, much less draw from it.

There really is no limit to the money you can have. This well will never run dry as long as you live. As I've hinted, however, getting you to believe that it is the one true source of your supply of money is the biggest challenge – and one I'm up for as long as you are willing to continue reading.

That's not much to ask for you to discover where an endless supply of fabulous wealth and riches lies, is it?

Well, you're still reading, so I'll keep my side of this bargain.

In order for you to be willing to look into and then draw money from this well, I need to get you to experience the riches it contains, so let me ask you a simple question.

The last time you went shopping for food, how much did you spend? I'm talking about your household groceries, not a special occasion or anything else. Now, I'm writing this in 2011. A week's shopping for my wife, me and our cat will cost us in the region of £50.

When I was a child in the 1960s my mother didn't work, (most married women didn't in those days), and my father brought home £14 a week. That money paid all the household bills, it bought a week's petrol and my father handed over all the remainder to my mother as "housekeeping" and she fed the four of us on that. We also managed two week-long family holidays a year.

My wife and I have conversations which are exact replicas of those I remember my parents having about things being "good value" or "a bargain" whilst others get mentally classified as "too expensive" or occasionally "a rip-off" if it seems too outrageous. And yet my parents would hardly be able to comprehend how much the actual cost of things has changed in half a century. You could buy a house in their day for what I can easily earn in a week now.

Does this mean that things are truly more expensive?

Now, I'm not going into economics here. What I want you to observe is that *money only has the meaning you give it.* The value of things is in your mind. It appears more "real" because there's a cultural, collective consensus on what constitutes good value or otherwise. (Economists call this "market forces" which is their gobbledygook for what people will pay for something. There's always a threshold beyond which they won't pay. If you want to see a microcosm of that, ask an auctioneer, or better still, check out Ebay and see what things that are plentiful sell for. Vitamins are a good example as there are always plenty for sale on Ebay. You may have the top brand or a unique blend but you still wouldn't be able to get much more for it than the current highest priced rival on the site.)

In other words, fifty years ago my parents would have had kittens at the thought of a week's groceries costing what would have then been about a month's entire pay! A hundred years ago the same money would have been closer to a year's salary!

Value and what things are worth are in the mind of the beholder.

So here's my kicker question: What are *you* worth?

No, I don't mean to sell you into slavery! I merely mean to enquire how much value you give? Not just in business but always and at all times? How much you are worth can really be measured by one simple thing: *it's what people say about you when you're not there!*

The only problem with that measurement is that you're never going to know for sure what it is. But no doubt you know, or have known, people whom you can't wait to see again or work with again. On the other hand, there'll have been a handful or maybe a barrow-load of those who get the sneers, the snide remarks and even ruder comments as soon as their back is turned.

You won't ever know, and there are unlikely to be many opportunities for you to even ask, but your job, if that's what you want to call it, is to leave the best impression possible wherever you go.

Does this mean being sycophantic, obsequious and a creep?

Absolutely not!

It means making people feel good by smiling, acknowledging their importance and significance, thanking them for their support, noticing their strengths and saying so. It means sometimes bringing a surprise cake or card to work, or giving your loved one flowers now and then for no reason other than that you thought about them and appreciated them.

It means coming from your heart, being joyful, letting others have their say – even if their views are diametrically opposed to yours – and being aware that without differences and contrasts your life would be very, very dull and empty.

It means coming from and exuding love.

It means being enthusiastic about your life – including your work.

It means being grateful and focusing on what's positive and what's working rather than what's not right.

All of which means you'll get to feel good almost all the time.

And more, much more than that, it means everyone and their dog will want a share of you because you make them feel so good. Which means they'll *pay* you to stick around!

The highest paid "commodity" or attribute in the world is *enthusiasm!*

Think about that. There are millions of chefs in the world, but only a handful of celebrity chefs. Is their food really so much better than all the Michelin starred chefs we've never heard of? Or even less decorated ones?

Of course not! There will be plenty of outstanding chefs, but the ones who make it to celebrity status have an extra *zing* to their personality.

How many celebrity gardeners can you think of?

In any field you care to name, it's the passion, the sheer love that can't be hidden for whatever it is these people do that gets them to the top of their particular tree.

Of course, I don't mean to suggest that success equals celebrity. It's just that we can observe the ones in the public eye so we can analyse to some degree why they are where they are.

Your skill and knowledge will, there's no question, open some doors and maybe get you through some job interviews. But skill and knowledge alone are not enough. If you are competing with other candidates who all have the same qualifications as you, how are the interview panel going to choose between you?

They're going to choose the one who makes them feel the best. That is the one they feel they could most comfortably get along with as a colleague.

It doesn't mean that you crack a rude joke at interview or that you play a prank on the boss! It means that you shine with the love you have for your life and for whatever field of work you are applying to work in. It isn't about necessarily being the best on paper; it's about being the best human being you can be.

## *Who To Work For*

Although I've been using illustrations that include job interviews I have another view to share regarding money and how to attract unlimited amounts of it.

What it amounts to is simply this: *Work for yourself.*

There are a number of reasons for this advice, even though I know not everyone will follow it. That's perfectly okay – some people are by nature better followers than leaders and even if you do form or run your own business you will need others to help you. However, please note the phrase "by nature." It is likely that as someone who has chosen to read this book – a book on self help – that your nature and your desire is to change some things in your life, one of which may well be your employment status. People who aren't looking for change aren't so likely to be reading this!

The first, but not the primary reason for the advice to work for yourself is that you'll never get rich working for someone else. Why is that not primary? Because chasing money for its own sake will leave you very hollow and empty indeed. It might make you unpopular too. I've already covered in some depth my explanation regarding attracting money by being attractive! That means, in a nutshell, aligning yourself with your passions and loving yourself and your life.

Money will come as a by-product of doing that.

The second, but probably the most important reason to work for yourself is therefore that when you are doing something you love you'll enjoy every moment of your life. Work will be synonymous with play in your world.

However, the old adage, "Do what you love and the money will follow" has some pitfalls that you should be aware of. The most important of these is that the money may not follow immediately!

## *What To Do For A "Living"*

The choice is simple: you can make a living or you can have a life. The secret here is that in that very innocuous looking heading, ("What to do for a living"), there's a trap.

You almost certainly won't have spotted it because the language is such common parlance that it passes all of us by unnoticed almost every time. Then again, since you know me quite well by now, perhaps you did.

The trap – and the key to the escape route – is in the verb "do." What you *do* shouldn't define you! And yet we ask almost instinctively as the ice-breaking question whenever we're introduced to someone new, "Hello. What do you do?"

Imagine if instead we were to ask, "What fascinates you?" Or, "What are you really passionate about?" Or even, "Is your life perfect yet? And if it isn't, what would make it that way?"

Wouldn't the ensuing conversations be far, far more interesting on the whole?

If you agree with me, then ask *yourself* those questions! Begin with asking this one, "How do I feel about what I do for a living?"

If the answer is in the region of "bored" or "frustrated" or anything negative that comes out on top then you have a decision to make. You must either find a way to enjoy it or get the hell out of there as fast as you possibly can. Which would mean tomorrow.

"Oh," you cry, "I couldn't possibly do that. I've got bills to pay, my kids to get through college and besides, I've got a big pension in just ten years' time."

Excuse me? Ten years, (not wishing to be blunt but hey, this is a self help book), is more than ten percent of most people's life spans. Are you really willing to sell ten years of your life for however much that pension will be?

And as for the expenses, when on earth did you pick up the notion that all your financial eggs have to be in that particular basket?

There are literally billions of (legal and ethical) ways to receive money. The internet is peppered with them – opportunities the like of which the world has not seen since the demise of the Wild West!

Just remember, as I said earlier, to ask yourself how you can *add value.* Don't try the useless "press a button and watch the cash roll in" scams. I have a friend who has a website about how to find free food by foraging in the hedgerows. He makes a *small fortune* from that website. I heard of a woman in the USA – a mother of school age children – who is pulling in thousands of dollars every month with her website of curtain making patterns – a skill she happened to be good at!

By the way, I'm not suggesting that all you need do is to put up a website about your hobby and watch the cash roll in either – you'll need some help (or knowledge) about how to get the customers, but all of it is very findable on the internet if you are interested and willing to do a little research. Really, a little – but not none!

All right, all right, I know this is hard line stuff. Impetuous job-quitting can lead to some scary consequences, although I've done it and survived and I know countless more people who have done the same and fared far better than me.

I want to make you think, though, about what you truly value. To my way of thinking, time is the only commodity you can never replace. If you're selling thirty-five to a hundred hours or even more every week to do something that drives you nuts in some way, then you are already nuts! That's a treadmill even a hamster would get off! You are, in that situation, effectively doing nothing more than marking time until the grave. I really don't believe that life is for that, and I know you don't either. If you did, you wouldn't be reading this.

## *A Simpler Way To Do It*

Here's a stark reality worth facing: If you're unhappy in your work and you leave, you'll only take *you* with you to the next place! Which is a round-about way of saying that happiness – and by default your unhappiness – is of your own creating.

Now, people don't like it when I say this because they think I'm saying "It's your fault." If that's your reaction let me tell you straight off the bat, you have the concept upside down. This isn't an accusation; it's a definition of your *power*. You can change the way you look at anything and when you do *everything* will begin to change around you.

Yes, this is both simple and powerful, but getting you to believe in it may not be such a simple task. That's because you're conditioned to want to know what to *do* to make this "work." In fact, if you've come across this type of concept before you may well be saying "I've *done* that and it didn't work."

The reason for that is that this has very little to do with "doing," and everything to do with "being."

Let me break that down for you. If you go to your kitchen now to make a cup of tea you will *do* a number of actions in a particular sequence to produce tea. You, however, will fundamentally stay the same throughout the process. It will not, unless you have some extraordinary relationship with tea, profoundly change you.

Admittedly, some tasks are considerably more complex than tea-making and will require that you learn skills above and beyond such basic kitchen ones as putting the kettle on.

But the principle in general remains the same: you do not change through what you do. It's the difference between someone asking "What do you do?" and "How do you do what you do?" To answer the second question you'd have to describe a state of *being*.

I've given the example elsewhere of having the experience of looking back on a once embarrassing moment and being able to laugh at it. The moment itself did not change; your perception of it did. That is an ability you have access to at any time. All you have to do is make it conscious and then learn how to bring it under your control.

In the case of work that you don't love you aren't going to wait for embarrassing moments! You are going to start noticing what there is to appreciate about it. No matter how bad you think it is, there will be things – in fact a plethora of things once you start opening up your mind.

Consider your colleagues: is there someone who is friendly with you, someone who makes you laugh or smile, (not in an unkind way at the expense of other people)? Is there someone who's helped you out of a pickle?

How about your environment? If you work indoors, it almost certainly keeps you warm and dry at the very least. Perhaps there's a decent brand of coffee available for your breaks. If you work outdoors, then you have some natural beauty to experience – even if you work somewhere smelly or dirty.

Come on! Work with me here! I don't know anything about you, your work or your complaints about it!

You could start with something really mundane, like perhaps the colour of the paint on the office walls if it happens to appeal to you.

Anything will do – just shift your focus.

Have you ever played that game where you are asked to look for everything brown around you? Try it now. Just take a moment wherever you are and look around you. Try, in thirty seconds, to notice as many brown things as you can. Small or large it doesn't matter.

Ready?

Go!

..... *30 seconds later* ....

Okay, now close your eyes and ....

...recall all the *blue* things you can.

I once led a workshop in a lovely country house on a gorgeous spring day. On a whim, I decided to send the participants for a walk, but not just any walk. I gave them specific instructions. They were not to speak, be led by their instincts, and be aware of what they noticed. They were to be back in exactly one hour and at the half way point, (wherever that was for them), they were to bring back the "gift" that they would find waiting for them there and then describe its meaning.

(The gift could be anything from a leaf to a stick, a pebble or even the view). They could go wherever they wished, but they were to walk in silence and alone. I set the exercise up to be a waking meditation, in other words.

When they returned and we'd all had some coffee, we set about sharing our experiences. Two participants, a man and a woman, had chosen the same woodland path as it happened.

When the woman described her journey, she talked of how the blossom seemed to be showing its colours just for her, how the sun warmed and delighted her, and how everything seemed to just fill her whole being, her very soul, with beauty and love.

The man spoke next, declaring first that he had walked down the same path, but he could not believe her experience.

His description of the journey began with snagging his trousers on the stile which was there, and continued with how he had been offended by noxious cow dung which he had narrowly avoided stepping in and the resultant army of flies. He went onto talk about a stone that had tripped him up, brambles that caught in his hair, and all in all what a thoroughly miserable time he had had!

Get clear about this: these were two people walking down the *exact* same path at the *exact* same time.

If that doesn't make my point clear, find a friend and repeat my experiment! You see what you expect to see. The man's life was filled with "problems" including, at the time, self esteem issues, and he had a tendency to blame anything and anyone.

The woman, by contrast, felt good about her life in general and was one of those people who would make the best of any situation.

If you are struggling to find something good about your work, boss or anything to do with your job, find someone who loves it and *interview them!* Buy them dinner as a bribe if you have to, but just get their take on how they experience work. You want to find out how they *do* happiness. And don't try and bring them down to your level by telling them how awful you find it! This person is your teacher – listen, watch and learn!

You can also shift the focus onto the other end of this particular spectrum: your role at work. Regardless of what you think your job is, or how you believe others perceive you, let me tell you what your real job is.

### Golden Key Principle: Your job is to bring joy!

That's it! Make people feel good. Make them smile. Pay them compliments. Thank them, praise them – yes the boss too. You will only be able to do this by making yourself feel good first, so you will have to do some major focus-shifting at both ends.

Just imagine how different things will feel when you shift from getting up for work like this:

*"Oh s\*\*t. Another day in that awful place. I hope so-and-so doesn't breathe down my neck today. Oh, and it's Monday and I have to do such-and-such on Mondays. No wonder they wrote that song about hating Mondays ..."*

To this:

*"How exciting – another day to experiment with ways I can make people feel good! The boss was never so shocked last week when I told him I like his tie. He actually smiled! But I really did – it's just that I've never said anything like that to him before! I noticed Susan was looking a bit glum on Friday. I'll make her coffee during our break today just as a token way of saying "I've noticed you." Oh, and I must thank Joe for fixing my computer mouse ..."*

The old fashioned word for this is "fun." You can have that anywhere. More important, you can *be* that all the time. It all adds value.

And now you know why your work has very little to do with what you *do*.

# 17: Health

Maybe I should have started the book with this chapter. After all, without your health you really have nothing. A billionaire who can barely breathe or get out of bed is hardly going to enjoy shopping trips or travelling!

However, I didn't start the book at this chapter for a couple of compelling reasons. Health is taken, by most of us, as a given and therefore for granted, unless it's not working too well. It's the underdog of the subject headings – most people are much more enamoured of wealth and happiness and success than they are with health! After all, when the wealth comes in, most of don't exactly celebrate with a healthy salad and a workout at the gym!

There is another reason why this chapter is deep within the book: I don't consider that I'm a great health expert, or at least I didn't until recently.

You see, I've always enjoyed good health. Perhaps I shouldn't have done. I smoked from the age of fourteen until I was thirty-six for a start. I lived on fried food and pasties when I was a student. I was drunk quite a bit when I was training as a nurse in the 1970s.

And yes, I developed a smoker's cough and I had hangovers from the drinking, but all of that healed.

My parents, on the other hand, were non-smoking, non-drinking vegetarians! (Yes, they get an exclamation mark because they were both born in the 1920s and lived through the war years when everyone smoked and not eating meat definitely marked you out as a weirdo!)

My mother died of cancer aged 40. My father dropped dead of a heart attack aged 73, although he was amazingly strong and robust until the day before his death.

Genetically, then, I don't have the best pedigree. Personally, I don't have a diet or exercise regime that qualifies me to tell you how or what to eat or how much to exercise your body.

But recently, I made a fantastic discovery. It was one of those moments when, once I'd seen this piece of wonderful news, it wasn't so much of an "Aha!" moment as an "I knew it all along!" one. The truth *feels* right.

The discovery is this: Our health depends far more on what we *believe* about what we eat and drink than it does on what we actually take in.

Try that idea on for size again. Your *beliefs* affect you and your body *more* than the food you eat!

Is this a license to go out and get drunk after a burger binge? No, of course not! Apart from anything else, there are far too many acknowledged and culturally held beliefs about what that would do to you for most people to be able to fly in the face of it. Besides, would it really feel good?

It is, however, freeing. You *can* eat and drink things if they genuinely feel good. (That doesn't just mean they *taste* good.) The key to staying healthy is therefore *awareness*.

In fact, you and the food need to feel good. I have more than one friend who has yo-yo dieted over the years. It's a nightmare.

I just love it when they're plump, but once the dieting starts again, oh my god!

"I like that but it's not included in my daily list of green okays/red sins…" or whatever the terminology of the day might be. Their food world becomes full of "shouldn'ts" and "mustn'ts" and the word "naughty" gets used a little too often. They start to lose the weight and although they enjoy their reflection better than before and the fact that some of their old clothes fit a little better, they're hardly happy.

They live in a perpetual state of guilt and angst, wishing they could have the things they've denied themselves and trying to convince themselves that the pound or three they've lost is well worth all the struggle.

Personally, I think we passed the point long ago where anyone should seriously believe that diets work. Diets don't work for a plethora of reasons, but the overriding one as far as I'm concerned is that you can't treat your body like a machine.

If your car develops a fault, with a bit of luck, (and a chunk of money in the bank), you can send it to a mechanic who will fix it for you. Your body doesn't work that way. You can't treat a few extra pounds as a "fault" and then expect that the "fix" is to start eating things you really don't want. Your car, as far as I know, has no emotional response to being fixed or faulty. You do, and you can't take that out of the equation!

Wrapped up in your diet and body image are all kinds of other factors, like your self esteem, what others may or may not think of you, how your lover responds to you, (if you have one), or how you rate your chances of getting one if you feel fat and ugly if you don't currently have one.

I keep coming back to the same message because the same conclusion seems unavoidable to me: you and the food have to feel good.

Or, to put it another way, *you* have to feel good.

I once attended a workshop led by Gill Edwards, whom I regard as a mentor of mine and whose first book, "Living Magically" opened my eyes to many ideas I might otherwise still be searching for.

At the time, Gill was touring a lot, delivering workshops about her gentle brand of metaphysics. Gill is very slightly built and was clearly a bundle of bright, sparkly and seemingly boundless energy. At some point in the proceedings she divulged that sometimes her only food would be chocolate biscuits which she would eat as she was driving between one venue and the next – sometimes a day long drive.

Several women in the room gasped and one of them asked her, "How come you're so slim?"

Gill replied that she *chose* to believe that the food her body wanted would nourish her and keep her healthy. Now, you can't just decide that chocolate biscuits are fine for you from now on. Gill was very in tune with her body and *aware*.

I recall asking her if she thought that smoking could be regarded in the same way. Her reply was fascinating. She pointed out that in our society we use tobacco smoke to "suck back in" emotions. The native American Indians who smoke a "peace pipe" (admittedly not twenty times a day), do not seem to be harmed by the tobacco smoke. But they believe it brings tranquillity and peace, not that it is a stress reliever.

Something to think about? Certainly there is room for some research there, but I doubt it will ever be done unless the tobacco companies feel that native American Indians are their last untapped market!

Please read what I am saying with great care. I am by no means advocating bad eating habits, and certainly I am not suggesting that it is okay to smoke. (I hate everything about smoking.) I am saying that it is our beliefs and feelings around what we put into our bodies, and how we treat them that make the most difference to how well we are.

Most of us who live in temperate countries like the United Kingdom, (as I do), or the United States or Europe would probably become ill if we were suddenly made to switch to the traditional diet of an Inuit. I don't think I would be very well on a diet of whale blubber! But they wouldn't do so well on salads either.

(Yes, I know there are environmental factors involved in that example.) The point I am trying to make is simply that there is not, and cannot be, a "one size fits all" diet for human beings.

Just to finish this particular point, I once read an article by the great anthropologist Desmond Morris who said that he teased his mother about her unhealthy diet as she served herself a full fried English breakfast. The joke was that his mother was ninety-nine years old at the time!

He went on to talk about how adaptable we are as a species. But he also made the point that his mother lived almost an entire century feeding herself on the principle that "if it tastes good, it is good." If she held that belief firmly enough, as she apparently did, then she seems to have been living proof of her own belief.

Your body is not fixed, it is fluid. Just to open up your mind on that a little, ask yourself where is the body that you had when you were a baby? Not one cell of it is here now, and the one you have now looks and feels considerably different!

In fact, there is hardly a single cell of the body you had seven years ago in existence today!

There are verifiable cases on record of people with multiple personalities where one personality has a different spectacle prescription from another. I have even heard of a case where one personality is diabetic whereas the others are not!

The same eyes! The same pancreas! In his groundbreaking book, "The Biology of Belief" Bruce Lipton, a cell biologist, once and for all explodes the long held scientific notion that our DNA is fixed. It isn't – it changes according to our beliefs!

The implications of this are vast, but for our purposes it removes any last excuse you may have harboured regarding your health. You can no longer say it's in your genes. It's irrelevant!

Yes, I know that there are some terrible diseases that are said to be hereditary, such as Huntingdon's Chorea, and I do not know where we are with the research into diagnoses such as that. I only know that the body is capable of repair well beyond our present level of understanding.

Gill Edwards, whom I mentioned just a few paragraphs ago, has recently published a book called "Conscious Medicine" which will bring you up to date with a lot of current thinking on this subject. Deepak Chopra's book, "Quantum Healing" is also a real eye-opener.

It is time to accept – or at least, if you are deeply sceptical, seriously consider – that the body is not a machine that houses a mind! You are a mind/body in much the same way that an apple tree is a tree/earth. You are one continuous energy process, not a bag of separate items which happens to have some kind of in-built computer!

Desmond Morris' mother was right in my view. (Also in his at the time, and he's a respected scientist). Her attitude to life and food was no doubt what kept her alive for ninety-nine years.

And every time I write a paragraph like the preceding one I mentally catch my breath! Suppose my readers all go on burger binges! And then I laugh to myself! Most of you would never do such a thing, but if you are tempted from time to time make absolutely certain that your mind set is one of pure fun and pleasure long before you get your order in! If you eat your food feeling guilty, shameful or in any way negative, I now firmly believe that you will do yourself more harm than the occasional burger and fries could ever cause you.

The same goes for exercise. I hate exercise. But I love to dance. I love to go for long walks in the beautiful countryside I am privileged to live in. I enjoy a game of table tennis and badminton. Oh! Guess what? Those things are, coincidentally, *exercising* me! I would never go out and do exercise for the sake of it. Very few things are more boring to my mind!

The same message, which I am now fretting is itself becoming boring, runs throughout this book. And many other books too, by the way. It is a very simple one indeed: do what feels good. Always, and about everything.

It is learning to listen, to really listen to those inner voices and nudges, and to sift the ones that come from your heart and soul, (God, Source, Higher Self, Universal Intelligence ... Come Up With Your Own Name For It!), from the ones that come from your ego.

Of course it is not going to be good to smoke cigarettes or to inject heroin into your system. You *know* that. That kind of idea may come from a different need – such as the need to be accepted, (find some different friends fast if that's the case!). Actually, Deepak Chopra has a very interesting take on drug addiction. He isn't condoning it of course, but he does suggest that the increase in it is because more people are seeking a way to experience their true selves – which is as a manifestation of Source or God-energy.

Drugs won't get you there, but there are a lot of people, addicts and non-addicts alike, who have long sensed that the waking consciousness we all accept as "everyday life" is far from all there is or what each of us is here to do.

*BE* true to yourself in all things and your good health is a given. If you have allergies or other conditions that currently limit your life, please try something life EFT, (Emotional Freedom Technique or tapping), even if you use conventional medicine too.

You cannot be separate from your mind or your emotions, so why do you think your body should be? It has been the "accepted" view for three or four hundred years, (although not by all cultures), and it is on the wane. People once held the notion that the Earth was at the centre of the Solar System but that finally was overcome with a new truth that in the end was plain for everyone to see. The separation of the body from the mind *must* end as a concept. It is, when you boil it down, utterly ridiculous as an idea.

Ultimately, as you can see, your health is primarily a state of mind – your mind.

The joy of this way of understanding life is that it takes very little effort to live this way. You simply follow what feels good, and what I've discovered is that the more I do that it not only becomes easier to do but life itself eases up.

Abraham Hicks, the non physical group of beings who speak such astonishing love and wisdom through the teachings of Esther Hicks, make a gorgeous point about time. They say that it is not that you don't have enough time to get all the things you want done, but that you do not have enough leverage on the time you have. In other words, if you could get to the results you want more easily and more quickly you would always have plenty of time.

Living from your heart accomplishes that at a stroke!

And now I ask you to imagine the knock-on effect on your health of getting things done without stress or fear, and of having more time to simply chill out, spend time with your loved ones or in nature, meditating and so on.

Can you see how this all knits together as one whole philosophy, just as your body, mind and the spirit you emanate from are one whole "process" – not an isolated individual standing tiny and alone against an uncaring and vast universe!

That thought alone should make you feel better!

And so with that, let us move on to the ultimate dual goal – that of being happy and successful. For that, you will need to read the next chapter...

# 18:  Happiness And Success

Originally I intended to write two separate chapters; one on happiness and another on success.  But when I started to think about it, could someone who is unhappy truly be called successful?

It depends, I suppose, on who's judging.  Anthony Robbins tells of a billionaire he had as a life coaching client.  It seems that this man had everything: in addition to several luxurious homes, complete with servants and several yachts he could choose to sail in, he also was in great health, happily married and had two gorgeous and successful daughters.

And yet, Robbins said, the man was miserable.  Even the great Tony Robbins was stumped for a while!  But eventually he hit on it: the guy was *bored*.  There were no challenges left for him.  As they worked together, Tony was able to help the man get his life back in balance.

Bill Gates could, conceivably, have fallen into this trap.  With his Microsoft empire having long ago made him the richest man alive, Bill certainly doesn't need to worry about working for money.  Instead, he now spends a great deal of his time on his charity work.

There is yet one more anecdote regarding Anthony Robbins I should share before we discuss this issue ourselves.  Asking an audience of more than a thousand people if anyone considered themselves successful, he deliberately picked on a man near the front whom he had every reason to suppose would answer in the affirmative.

Robbins knew that the man was rich, with a thriving business, a happy marriage, great health – the complete package. So he confidently pointed at this man from the stage and asked him directly, "You, sir. Are you successful?"

To his astonishment the man said no. When Robbins asked him why, the man explained that he believed truly successful people had a higher net worth than he personally had, (his was measured in millions of dollars), a better body mass index, (his was close to champion athlete standard), and so on. He had a list of "rules" that made him feel he was still an underachiever and which also drove him harder and harder – unable to relax despite the outward appearance of success.

As you may imagine, the audience gasped. So Robbins asked for anyone else. A very enthusiastic man half way back in the auditorium could barely contain himself. He was jumping up and down like an over-enthusiastic schoolboy, thrusting his hand in a jutting motion towards the ceiling and yelling, "Me! Me!"

Picking up on this rampant enthusiasm, Robbins asked him how he knew he was successful.

"It's easy," said the man. "I think every day above ground is a successful day, and everything else is a bonus!"

Wow! If you make *that* your philosophy then every day is certainly going to seem like a party.

I have a friend who lives like that. He is the life and soul of any party. He turns dull gatherings into parties. He doesn't smoke or drink and certainly never takes drugs. If anyone says he should have a drink to "be sociable" he'll quickly and humorously remind them that he *is* being sociable. It's people who are sociable, he says, not drinks. And he's right.

As for drugs, he values life too much to want to compromise it and he's *always* high – on life!

And guess what? He's very successful! Success "happens" to him. His name is Jason Vale, aka "The Juice Master". You can look him up on Google – he has written some excellent books on natural health and juicing especially. If you are lucky enough to attend one of his workshops or retreats you will not only have the time of your life at the event – you will emerge with so much vitality for the rest of your life you'll feel like you'd been sleeping before! No, I'm not on commission. I just love the guy – his joyful, positive energy is infectious.

You know by now, unless you've skipped the whole of this book and jumped right onto this page, that success is a state of mind. Personally, I don't believe you are successful if you are also unhappy. You can also substitute "stressed" or "fearful" or "phobic" or "neurotic" or any other synonym for unhappiness you care to insert into the previous sentence – it all boils down to the same thing.

What is the point of collecting a lot of material paraphernalia if you are always fretting you could lose it, or you cannot leave the office before midnight? No one is going to stand at your grave side and praise you for your bank balance! Your legacy will be in terms of how good you made others feel. If you always have a smile, time to listen, make a great cup of tea … those are the sorts of things you'll be remembered for!

I'm all for material trappings – nice cars, luxury holidays and beautiful homes can be delightful, but not if they come at the expense of strained relationships with family and friends, mental and/or physical disease or other discomforts.

I trust, then, that we're agreed that happiness, and indeed success, are states of mind. However, the promise of this book is that you can have what you want whether or not you believe in the law of attraction, so let me give you a very practical, easy-to-make "recipe" to make happiness and success work pretty much every time.

## The Happiness And Success Recipe.

When most people encounter a challenge in their lives the first thing they tend to do is to label it a "problem." Can we knock that one on the head once and for all?

A "problem" used to be a mathematical conundrum set by our very unpopular maths teacher which forced us unfortunate boys to try to work out the angle a ladder was leaning against a wall, or what the arc of a thrown cricket ball would have to be to hit the wicket or some such useless thing.

These are not the kinds of issues that affect our lives for the most part, unless you are a maths teacher with a sadistic streak, a schoolchild with no head for geometry or an engineer, in which case it should be "bread and butter" to you anyway!

What does affect us are issues concerning our relationships, jobs, finances and so on, and along with all of those, our self esteem and beliefs regarding whether or not we feel we're up for those challenges.

Everything I've said and taught you in this book so far has to work in the "real world" too, of course. I can't have you reading this and saying, "Yeah, but you don't know about *my* situation."

Listen. Everybody thinks their situation is the one with no solution. And everybody would be wrong. There is nothing you haven't sorted or solved in your life so far or you simply wouldn't be here!

You know how to put yourself in any state you desire now, (re-read my instructions if you haven't been doing it). Adopt the belief that maybe – at least *maybe* – there is a way to achieve anything you desire. That's your starting point.

If you still find yourself resisting that idea with that annoying inner voice telling you that you can't, or people like you just don't... or whatever, then you can do two things.

First, change the voice. (I showed you how to do this in the state management process).

And second, ask yourself one simple question: *Is that true?*

You really have to answer that honestly. Is that absolutely, one hundred percent guaranteed true? I mean, you could assure anyone, under any circumstances, even if a gun was held to your head, that no matter what you cannot achieve such and such a thing or make the required change. Could you? If you answer yes I get to pull the trigger!

Hmm. So, hopefully, you've now arrived at a point where you are saying, "Well, if you put it *that* way, I suppose under *those* conditions, just *maybe* ..."

That's enough. That's all you need. It *may not* be true.

I don't need you to prove it to me one way or the other. But the first thought, that it is true that you could not achieve a thing, gives you no hope. The thought that there maybe a way that you could opens the door for some hope.

Why would you choose a hopeless thought over a hopeful one? You can choose your thoughts, remember?

That simple process does away with almost all resistance to most things in a flash. You can open yourself up to the possibility of success in anything – relationships, weight loss or body building, achievement in business, sport or creative arts, healing from diseases, (even the ones the doctors tell you are incurable or "you just have to live with!") Every day people are "healing" from "incurable" diseases. A lot of scientists will say this is not possible and dismiss the evidence as fraudulent or unacceptable because it can't be repeated.

*That doesn't mean it isn't valid.*

You will have to decide on which of these avenues to explore for yourself. I just want to open your mind to the notion that there are many, many things that in my half century on the planet alone are now possible that were considered impossible – *in my lifetime!*

It used to be considered impossible for anyone to run a mile in under four minutes – until Roger Bannister did it.

It was considered impossible to fly – until the Wright brothers did it.

It was deemed impossible to mass produce the motor car – until Henry Ford did it …

(No – none of those are within my lifetime! They are additional examples, okay?)

I will tell you this, though. Not one of those things would have been possible if the person or people concerned had not believed they were before they set out to turn their respective visions into the realities we now take for granted.

What do you consider impossible for yourself? Will you now begin to dare to dream?

Good!

Once you start the dreaming you are on the way. Now you have to choose your outcome.

Simply explore, in your mind, how you and your life will be different when the change is made. When it's all in place and done and dusted.

Imagine it vividly, as though you are writing a screenplay for a movie or telling the story to children. How do things look? Where do you live? (Is it different from where you live now?) *How* do you live? Has your appearance changed? And so on.

Take ten or fifteen or more minutes to really explore the world you want to create for yourself. As you do that, *feel* how it feels to inhabit that world. Enjoy this virtual reality you are creating in your mind. Your imagination is a muscle that probably has been dormant since you were aged less than ten!

But it is a very powerful tool indeed. As far as I know, no other species has such a faculty, so what is it for? From a Darwinian, (survival of the fittest) perspective it hardly seems necessary. Even the great apes, intelligent as they are, don't seem to think,

"I wonder what it would be like to make a hut out of all this mud," do they?

Human imagination is the reason we no longer live in caves! We cannot *not* imagine things – and those who allow their imaginations a little house room soon find that they can turn their dreams into reality.

When Disneyworld was first opened, Walt Disney himself had already passed away. It fell to his brother, Roy, to declare the new wonder open to the world. Allegedly, a journalist, who somewhat annoyed Roy Disney, asked him how it felt that Walt had not seen Disneyworld.

Roy is said to have retorted, "Walt saw every bit of this! If he hadn't, you and I wouldn't be standing here today!"

He may not have seen it completed, but Walt Disney's vision changed the modern world and children's entertainment forever. That's quite a legacy.

The more you live in your imaginary world, the more your external world will start to reflect it.

I know, if you're still cynical about the law of attraction, that you have some doubts about that last statement. If that's the case I issue you with a simple challenge: live it for a month – just thirty days. That means taking time out of your day – (you can always use your daily commutes to and from work if you have one), to exercise your imagination and feel how good it feels to live in the world you would love to create for yourself.

Thirty days. Here is the *least* that will happen. You will feel good every day for thirty days at least during those fifteen to twenty minute periods. Big deal!

Here is what is more likely to happen. You will get addicted to feeling good! You'll do it more than I've prescribed. You will find people, things and opportunities just showing up "out of the blue" that seem to open doorways to what you want.

I don't care if you're cynical. Try it – it works anyway!

Finally, take *action* – but be careful here! I don't mean that you should work your socks off. I fell into that trap for a long time. I thought I could imagine something as "so" and then I had to beaver away at it until it took shape. The old "keep your nose to the grindstone" mentality our forefathers handed down!

That kind of action will – or may – produce results, but it's the slow boat to China at best and a hiding to nothing at worst. The actions you need to take have to come from exactly the same place as everything else you've been doing if you've been following my guidance up to now: from your heart!

Actions have to feel good first! Working all the hours God sends doesn't feel good to me! You must trust in the fact that it isn't effort that pays off – it's belief in yourself. It's belief too that help will show up when you live from that place. That takes some trust until you get used to it, but then so did the idea that you could hurtle around the highways in a metal box without coming to harm when you first were learning to drive! It's worth getting used to – because you will feel good and your life will change for the better forever.

I know I keep reiterating that promise, but that's because the one thing I cannot do for you through the medium of a book is to prove it. Only you can do that.

I hope I have been persuasive enough for you to want to try it as a way of life. That is, being first, doing second.

*Be* happy, *be* loving, *be* successful … or whatever you want to *be* … in your mind and heart *first*.

Then, only then, will what to *do* bubble to the surface – and the more exciting the idea feels, the more reason for you to follow it. And follow it quickly! Don't hesitate and procrastinate and analyse it all to see why it won't work and why you could never … blah, blah, blah … back into the old way of being you will get sucked!

Act on feeling and feel good first.

That's your motto.

It works.

Try it.

Have a great life.

# Afterword: What If It Doesn't Work?

Every January, tens of thousands of people will join gyms fully intending to get in shape. This year they're *determined*. But we all know that a huge percentage of them will rarely if ever use their year's membership beyond February or March at the outside.

Good business for the world's gyms, but not exactly great for the health of all those well-intentioned people.

We could blame the gyms. They don't provide enough incentive perhaps. They could take more trouble to send out reminders. Or something else. But it isn't really the fault of the gyms, is it? They're just businesses, and if their paying customers choose to pay for a service that they don't take advantage of, it's no skin off the gym owners' noses. That's harsh I know, but I just want to make a point here; this isn't a treatise on business ethics!

Okay then. Let's blame the people. Perhaps the members who stop going are intrinsically lazy. That argument doesn't hold up to much scrutiny since they weren't lazy in January or February were they?

Maybe "human nature" kicks in and the majority of people fall back on the path of least resistance. It's simply easier not to make regular tips to the gym. I have to tell you I'm *allergic* to arguments citing "human nature" as the "cause" of anything. The ultimate expert on human nature has yet to be born and it certainly isn't anyone who is basing their so-called facts on what are nothing more than casual observations which reflect their own less than desirable character traits!

Rampage over…

What is the difference between someone who wants to get in shape and the person who becomes Mr. or Miss Universe for example?

Let's demolish these arguments and get to the core of the issue. In every field of human endeavour there are those who succeed at a very high level – let us call them the "gold medallists." And then there are those who are close on their heels, perhaps even inspired by them. For our purposes we can call them the bronze and silver medallists and all the also-rans. There's no shame in being twelfth or twentieth fastest or best at something in the world, is there? It's just that if you happen to be an Olympic athlete no one will remember your name ten minutes from now. Apart from your mother. But your achievement is still amazing!

Then there will be the vast majority who will be good but not good enough to be world class. To continue our metaphor, these will be the good and enthusiastic club players, but not the people we see on the world stage. That's fine too.

At the bottom of this particular ladder are the whingers – those who wish they could but believe they can't. Believe them, they've tried.

Now those are the people who give up their gym attendance. What's going on?

If you re-read the scene I set at the top of this chapter you'll see that their way was paved with good intentions. They started off "determined" to get in shape in my example. This kind of gritted teeth approach won't work.

Put all of this in the context of this entire book. I've done my utmost to get across the simple singular point that it is *being* not *doing* that gets results! Willpower is not going to work because willpower is not intended for this kind of purpose.

## *The Abuse Of Willpower*

To see what I mean let's quickly look at two areas where willpower is often put forward as the necessary prerequisite to success, namely dieting and quitting smoking.

In the vast majority of cases, what happens when anyone attempts these (seemingly) difficult feats, their mindset on approaching the task is once again grim determination. They prepare themselves for battle, (with whom?), and expect it to be difficult. These expectations can be magnified many times if the individual has made previous "failed" attempts, so the very least you and I could do is admire them for their courage!

But it's futile and utterly unnecessary.

The dilemma faced by both dieters and would-be non-smokers is the same in both cases. They know *intellectually* that they need to make drastic changes but *emotionally* they still want their "fix." The "battle" then is between head and heart.

Now, let's look at what happens in a situation where head and heart align. Suppose you're out shopping one day and you something you'd really love, but it's rather expensive. You will have to use your own imagination to fill in the blank here – for me it's a rather gorgeous computer, but for you it might be a dress!

So now your heart is set on getting the object of your desire and your head is saying, "it's too expensive." And now your heart says, "Can we find a way?" Suddenly you remember that dusty old wotnot that you've been meaning to sell on Ebay for years, or the advert you saw in your local post office that someone is offering to pay for a spot of gardening or dog walking …

Again, I could go on making up examples forever. But that won't get us to the point - which I'm sure you've got by now. When you're truly motivated, *inspiration strikes* and taking the follow-up actions becomes easy and even fun. Your willpower now becomes a useful tool that helps you to follow through on the actions you're already inspired to take. It should be obvious that anything that feels like a battle – with a part of yourself or anything else for that matter – isn't right.

You can take the attitude that the ideas in this book are just like everything else you've ever heard on this subject – and just as useless. If that's your starting point then if you try out anything I've suggested that would be a minor miracle in itself, but you will certainly do so with gritted teeth a heavy heart and a lot of resistance in your head.

Frankly, I'd say don't bother!

But you're almost at the end of the book so I doubt that's your attitude.

It's more likely that you still *want* it to work.

And now we come to that little word: "*it.*"

There really isn't an "it" you know! There's me, the author putting forward a set of ideas. And there's you the reader who will interpret my ideas in whatever way you will. Just as I have no control over that, you had no control over the content of this book, most of which you've now read.

If you consider it carefully, you'll see there's a triad – a three way relationship going on. You, me and the ideas in this book. No "it."

To make the ideas work you have to try them, and I'd seriously propose, should you have any shred of doubt or cynicism about the results you may or may not get, (and I wouldn't hold that against you), that you remember that the worst that can happen is that you get to feel good – a lot.

If feeling good about yourself and your life on a day to day basis holds no appeal for you then I guess you are sunk from the start! And don't come back at me saying that there's too much suffering in the world and that this kind of Pollyanna-ish attitude is selfish. That kind of martyrdom won't cut any ice with me! I've said elsewhere that you can't get poor enough to solve poverty or sick enough to end disease. And you certainly can't suffer enough to end suffering.

Your being stuck in misery of any kind serves no one. That's a kind of mental self-flagellation that doesn't belong in the twenty-first century, but if that is your line of thinking I can only plead with you to stop it immediately and never indulge in it again.

Most people, however, don't feel this way. Feeling good on purpose will not only have astounding results for you, but it is the perfect expression because of the duality of its meaning. Feeling good will also keep you "on purpose." In other words, you will increasingly often and with ever-more ease find yourself knowing what you want and where you're going. The way of getting there will also reveal itself.

And so we have come full circle. These ideas work, but if they are to work for you then you will need to choose how to *be* before you start *doing* anything with them. I'd recommend that you put yourself in a state of "playfulness" or "having fun" and then just lightly tickle these ideas.

You're feeling good already, aren't you?

Enjoy the journey! That's a wish from the heart not only for your journey through the experiment of putting this book's ideas into action, but for your life's journey too. That is how it is supposed to be.

# ABOUT THE AUTHOR

## *Who Am I To Tell You How To Live?*

In writing this book I feel I may have been somewhat audacious. Here I am, a middle-aged man whom you wouldn't particularly notice in a crowd telling you how you can have the three most valued things in life – health, wealth and happiness.

Do you remember how our children's fairy stories all end with, "And they lived happily ever after ..."

The Prince and the Princess overcome some serious obstacles, like being turned into a frog or sleeping for a century or so, find "true love" and marry. Those fairy stories never tell us how they paid the bills or who did the washing up or if they ever had an argument. "Happily ever after..." is such a blissful phrase and makes life sound like a dream, a utopia.

And yet I am not being audacious! I *am* living happily ever after as I write. I have a gorgeous wife who is always "sunny side up" – and we are very much in love. We have never argued about a bill or the washing up, and though there have been moments when a cross word has been exchanged, it has always died away in an instant or two. We love each other – and the life we have together – too much to waste it fighting. We laugh a lot.

My own parents, by contrast, had rows that could last for days. My mother would go into long silences and not speak to my father for literally three days at a time if she was upset enough with him. My father too had a fearsome temper, which though not often shown, was like a volcanic eruption when he did "blow." My life, and way of life, is a million miles from that.

My health, as I have mentioned elsewhere, is great. I am no athlete, and I confess to only intermittent bouts of exercise. But I am hardly ever ill and I have plenty of energy.

As for money, I have more than enough and my personal wealth is increasing almost daily as I write this.

None of these things came easily to me. I have hacked my way through the jungle of life to find the keys to love and financial well being for sure. I had to find my own sense of self-worth first which took me until well into my thirties.

Next, I had to figure out whether I could entertain the idea, once it had been shown to me, that we create our own reality. The "billiard ball" model of how things are was much easier for me to accept. It went something like this: the red ball falls into the pocket because it has been struck by the white ball which in turn was struck by the cue which was being held by the player who made a conscious decision to hit the ball …

Cause and effect. Simple, measurable Newtonian physics. The mystery had long ago been solved.

Yet it wouldn't do. There were too many unanswered questions for me. How did the snooker player make the decision to strike the ball in that particular way? Why does he get pleasure from playing at all? (It's hardly a survival instinct at work!) And on and on – with many questions such as the ones I've already addressed throughout this book.

Of course, it wasn't billiards or snooker I was concerned with. It was my own life. I had either turned up at random into a random world where death and eternal oblivion are the only certainties, or I had not. If not, then there was some consciousness behind my having "occurred" into the world – but whose? Mine or God's? And if there was a God, what use was he, she or it to me? If there wasn't, why didn't I have any recollection of wanting to get here, and how come I'd chosen – if chosen I had – such a messy and often miserable start to my life?

I could accept that I was part of a system. I couldn't live without sun or air any more than I could without water or food, and so the air, the sun and even gravity were "part" of me, even though I had the experience that I begin and end at my skin.

As time passed, I came also to accept that I, and everyone else, was malleable. It is obvious, with only a little thought, that no one remembers everything. Can you recall what you had for breakfast on the fifteenth Thursday of 2001? The memory is apparently stored in there somewhere but most of us don't care so we aren't conscious of that memory.

When we tell someone who we are, it's as though we produce a slide show of our life, picking out what we have deemed significant events that then explain to ourselves and others how come we've turned out the way we have. People also use some of those memories as excuses for not changing. "I can't help the way I am … because XYZ happened to me when I was a child…"

Once I realised that I could pick any memories, and furthermore, via my NLP training, discovered that I could also change the way I felt about any event that surfaced in memory, it was clear to me that I could turn out any way I wanted.

One of the lessons in "A Course In Miracles" simply says, "I can choose peace rather than this."

I got that. I can choose *anything* rather than something that disturbs or hurts me, so why wouldn't I exercise such a choice?

*Why wouldn't I exercise such power?*

Why wouldn't anyone?

And hence began my journey of change and self discovery, but most of all, to my discovery of the keys to happiness, health and wealth. And yes, I know I've put those in a different order to the more common, "health, wealth and happiness," but they are now in logical order.

If you are unhappy on a regular or consistent basis, sooner or later that is going to show up in your body and your health will be compromised. As for wealth, whether in material or spiritual form, it will not cling to you or make you feel good if your general disposition is miserable and negative.

To say, "I am by nature a worrier" or to label yourself with any such negative thought is not only self destructive, but also unnecessary and fundamentally untrue.

You are by nature a mini-god who may not be able to dictate the weather but who is endowed with infinite power to decide how to react to it

Life is lived, I have discovered and I can tell you unequivocally, from the inside out. Most of us have been taught to behave as if it was the other way around – in other words, from the outside in.

If you adopt that idea, then your happiness depends on a myriad conditions being just so – from how you are taxed to the mood your spouse got out of bed in this morning, the weather, your in-laws, your teenage children ... the list would literally be endless.

Your happiness will be rare and fleeting indeed.

I recently heard a very successful internet marketer, (of all people!), say this in a talk he gave:

"I hate most internet marketing. The only kind that I am interested in is the kind that delivers value. I live from the principle of giving more than I get – and that is why I am so successful."

His name, should you be interested to check him out, is Jason Fladlien. He teaches internet marketing, but he also teaches how to live. There are some good guys out there!

I too have come to see and believe that I have the ability and the right to teach people how to live. Not because I want to dictate or control, but from a desire to free each spirit to follow their own dreams and hearts as I yearned to do for myself for much of my early life.

The alternative, to not getting this message out, as I see it, is to allow millions of people to continue to live with a fundamental belief in hopelessness. There is nothing we can do about war or global warming or the neighbours' cat ... this is all nonsense.

For every person who really gets that by living as givers and as choosers of our state at every and any moment, the world will improve as each person naturally, by default and without effort, pays that forward.

That is why I have written this book and why I will continue to deliver messages of hope and self empowerment until my time here, in this particular form, comes to an end.